MW01136226

BEST GOURMET RECIPES

The purpose of this book is to provide recipes and instruction
in preparing foods that are good for your health and
taste wonderful too! The recipes are based on
pure vegetarian or vegan principles. They
contain no meat or dairy products, table
sugar or highly refined products
and are sweetened principally
with fruit products.

by Neva Brackett
Fourth Edition©, 2002
Reno, Nevada

Best Gourmet Recipes
P.O. Box 10730
Reno, Nevada 89510
Phone # available on this website:
WWW.BestGourmetRecipes.org

BEST GOURMET RECIPES

The purpose of this book is to provide recipes and instruction
in preparing foods that are good for your health and
taste wonderful too! The recipes are based on
pure vegetarian or vegan principles. They
contain no meat or dairy products, table
sugar or highly refined products
and are sweetened principally
with fruit products.

by Neva Brackett
Fourth Edition©, 2002
All rights reserved
Reno, Nevada

SPECIAL THANKS

There are so many who have contributed to the success of this book we are hesitant to share names but at least I want to mention those of our many cooks at Five Loaves who through the years have experimented with foods, and then tried them out on our customers who continually inspire us.

Our special appreciation for culinary skills goes to Francis Atkins, Kim Berg, Kathy Coleman, Milca and Ed Dominado, Jim Goodwin, Bryant Griffin, Charles Hernandez, Darleen Hillebert-Ames, Elizabeth Hoeg, Darlene Lind, Mitch McCain, Darryl Price, Ron and Maribeth Simkin, David Whitford, and Lance Williams. We also give our gratitude for the many volunteer hours given by proofreaders Frances Foster, Phyllis Glantz, Gerita Liebelt, Suzan Pendleton and Donna Pihl.

A special word of appreciation also to our daughters, Kathy and Kimberley, who have spent summers and vacations working hard in the restaurant, even bringing their friends to help and inspire us with their fresh ideas and enthusiasm. Kimberley was the principal food stylist for all our beautiful pictures.

I also want to thank my good friend Rilla Klingbeil who was the cooking school instructor at Weimar Institute and shared her knowledge with Kimberley who brought it home to us. Many of her recipes became stand-by's in the restaurant and our book wouldn't be complete without them.

Our very special thanks also to Yolanda Leamon who has provided such wonderful inspiration for good health and whose enthusiam for the restaurant ministry led us to open Five Loaves. She has done more than any other person to promote this book and has contributed some fifteen plus recipes to help fill in some special needs for the North American Division heart-health program of which she is a co-developer.

Then, of course, there's Evelyn Earl, my mother-in-law, who co-authored *Something Better** with me and continued to share recipes and ideas which are part of this book. My own mother and sister also have contributed recipes and encouragement.

And then there is my dear husband, who, in reality, co-authored this book, did all the photography, design, computer layout and most of the printing of the first edition.

But above all, I owe my deepest debt of gratitude to the One who bid us, "Give ye them to eat."

*Cookbook first published in 1979, third edition in 1985

"Not unto us, O Lord, not unto us, but unto Thy name give glory, for Thy mercy , and for Thy truth's sake." *Psalm* 115:1

CONTENTS

WHAT IS FIVE LOAVES?

It is a restaurant-bakery-deli in Seattle that offers foods that are both wholesome and palatable. We select our ingredients from the vast variety of foods as they are grown, using no animal products and avoiding highly refined foods.

WHO OWNS AND OPERATES FIVE LOAVES?

During it's first ten years of operation, Five Loaves was owned by the Seventh-day Adventist churches in Western Washington. The mission statement was to improve health through better nutrition and help those interested find a right relationship with their Creator to be prepared for His soon return to this earth.

HOW DOES ONE KNOW WHOM TO BELIEVE IN MATTERS OF HEALTH?

This is a very pertinent question for anyone who has ever stood in front of the intriguing, and sometimes confusing array of books on display in the health section of today's book stores. So many differing ideas are being promoted—macrobiotic, lacto-ovo vegetarian, vegan, raw foods, vitamins, herbs, barley green, wheat grass, "live" foods, high protein—this is just the beginning! What is the right course? We pick up a book promoting barley green and begin to read. It sounds so convincing as we read the testimonies of how plants and people are greatly benefited by this product. Then we pick up a book on food combinations. Someone is promoting the importance of not eating proteins with fruits, and certain foods must be taken in the right order for the greatest benefit to our digestion.

Our understanding on these matters is found in a question: "Would not the Creator who made us and longs to communicate His truth to us wish to lead us out of this confusing maze of information?" King David wrote, "I waited patiently for the Lord; and He inclined unto me and heard my cry. He brought me up also out of a horrible pit, out of the miry clay, and set my feet upon a rock, and established my goings." *Psalm 40:1,2.* "Bless the Lord, O my soul... Who satisfieth thy mouth with good things so that thy youth is renewed like the eagle's." *Psalm 103:1,5.*

Unknown to many, the Bible contains much information on the subject of health. Seventh-day Adventists have also had great confidence in the writings of Ellen G. White, a late 19th century author who seemed clearly inspired on various subjects of Christian living. Many were naturally skeptical of her "inspiration" at first, but as they compared her teachings with the Bible they found harmony and their confidence in her teaching grew. She wrote widely on "health reform," and the passing of years has confirmed the validity of her concepts. We have referenced some of her suggestions in *Best Gourmet Recipes*—we believe you'll find them helpful.

As a result of her writing, Seventh-day Adventists began, in the late 1800's, teaching the value of a vegetarian diet and other aspects of healthful living. By the turn of the century the Adventist church was operating sanitariums, hospitals and vegetarian restaurants around the country as a means of teaching good health principles.

FOREWARD

These were new to many of that day when blood-letting and poisonous drugs were standard medical treatments. Instead of "purifying" the system by blood-letting, and keeping patients confined to beds in stuffy rooms, Adventist physicians taught the importance of free circulation of the blood through exercise in the fresh air. Instead of the frequent administration of strong drugs, the immune system was stimulated into action by the use of hydrotherapy—hot and cold water treatments. Patients were fed a vegetarian diet and given regular periods of exercise in the sunshine—these were considered *nature's* "doctors."

In reality, this was all the result of Ellen White's inspired writing. Among the books written by her on the subject of health were *The Ministry of Healing* and *Counsels on Diet and Foods*. These may be obtained from Five Loaves or the local Adventist Book Center. Call 1-800-253-3000 for the one nearest you.

IS SCIENCE A VALID SOURCE OF INFORMATION CONCERNING HEALTH?

"God is as truly the author of physical laws as He is author of the moral law. His law is written with His own finger upon every nerve, every muscle, every faculty, which has been entrusted to man." *Counsels on Diet and Foods,* p. 17.

Building on the accumulated knowledge of previous scientific discovery, there is a wealth of information today concerning human physiology. Truly, God's perfect order can be seen in nerves and cells of the body. This knowledge allows evaluation of the validity of much of the health literature being sold to the public today. An understanding of the specific function of enzymes, vitamins, proteins, fats, and carbohydrates in cellular metabolism makes clear what is needed in our diet.

"God has formed laws which govern our constitutions, and these laws which He has placed in our being are divine, and for every transgression there is affixed a penalty, which must sooner or later be realized. The majority of diseases which the human family have been and still are suffering under, they have created by ignorance of their own organic laws. They seem indifferent in regard to the matter of health, and work perseveringly to tear themselves to pieces..." *Counsels on Diet and Foods,* p.19.

HOW CAN MY DIET AFFECT MY RELATIONSHIP WITH THE CREATOR?

The answer to this question is illustrated by the effect of alcohol on the mind. In the bloodstream, alcohol causes red blood cells to become sticky and clump together, clogging capillary blood flow. The brain is first to suffer. The fine-tuned ability of discretion is lost and the affected person speaks and acts in ways that would likely bring embarrassment if the mind was clear!

Could it be that overeating, a high fat diet and a sedentary lifestyle similarly dull the mind, perhaps only slightly, making it difficult for one to discern right from wrong and to appreciate Christ's sacrifice on Calvary?

The Bible says, "Taste and see that the Lord is good." One can put this to the test for themselves. Try it for 10 days: start with a pleasant walk in the fresh air using that time to meditate

FOREWARD

and commune with the One who made us. Then eat a hearty breakfast, a wholesome dinner, and light supper with no snacking between meals. Your experience will likely confirm the validity of these principles we call nature's doctors under the acronym of NEW START: Proper NUTRITION, EXERCISE, the use of adequate WATER, exposure to SUNLIGHT, TEMPERATE living, fresh, pure AIR, adequate REST and TRUST in Divine power.

WHAT DOES TAKING CARE OF MY HEALTH HAVE TO DO WITH JESUS' SOON COMING?

"And this gospel of the kingdom shall be preached in all the world for a witness unto all nations; and then shall the end come." *Matt. 24:14*

Jesus taught that His "Gospel" was to be given to all the world before He comes the second time. "Gospel" means "good news." Jesus came to teach the truth about God, and as His witnesses we are privileged to do the same. The last book of the Bible describes in more detail what that gospel is that will be given before He comes:

"And I saw another angel fly in the midst of heaven, having the everlasting gospel to preach unto them that dwell on the earth... saying with a loud voice, Fear God, and give glory to Him: for the hour of His judgment is come: and worship Him that made heaven, and earth, and the sea, and the fountains of waters." *Revelation 14:6,7.*

1. We are to give glory to God. Taking care of our body and keeping it in good health has much to do with giving glory to God: "What? know ye not that your body is the temple of the Holy Ghost which is in you, which ye have of God,

and ye are not your own? For ye are bought with a price: therefore glorify God in your body..." *1 Corinthians 6:19,20.*

2. We are to worship Him who made heaven and earth. We are not told to worship the things He made, but to worship the One who made them. When God made the first man and woman, he gave to them their diet—fruits, grains, and nuts. Later, vegetables were added. We believe we can honor our Creator best by returning as nearly as possible to that original diet given by Him to the human race.

OUR PERSONAL EXPERIENCE

Our family has been greatly blessed by following these principles. Our daughters, raised from birth as vegetarians (vegans, in reality) are healthy, happy, in service for mankind and making significant contributions to society. When my husband introduces our daughters and me at his speaking engagements, he teases me and the audience by saying, "I don't want you to be confused about which of these ladies is the mother!" In reality, I'm a 50 plus grandmother now, but I've never felt better or enjoyed better health than I do today.

We wish above all things that you can share this experience with us—that's why Five Loaves was established and why we share the wonderful recipes from our kitchen. We hope you enjoy them and find them a great blessing for your own physical and spiritual health.

INTRODUCTION

Welcome to the recipe section of this book! We trust you will find many happy results from your search through these pages. Our philosophy for better health has been shaped by various scientific achievements, by the Holy Scriptures and from the very practical counsel of a widely quoted health advocate from yesteryear, Ellen White. We hope the nuggets from these sources will inspire you as much as they have us!

"Again and again I have been shown that God is trying to lead us back, step by step, to His original design,—that man should subsist upon the natural products of the earth."

Counsels on Health, p. 451

Spinach Crepes, Potato Patties and Scrambled Tofu

A ccording to the new food pyramid, fruits and grains should compose the major part of our diet. Fruits, grains, and nuts were the original diet given to man by the Creator. Therefore, the custom of starting the day with cereal and fruit is a good step in the right direction, but why get it refined, enriched, and sugar-coated out of a box? Here are some wholesome breakfast ideas that will help you start your day right.

"In grains, fruits, vegetables, and nuts are to be found all the food elements that we need. If we will come to the Lord in simplicity of mind, He will teach us how to prepare wholesome food free from the taint of flesh meat." *Counsels on Diet and Foods,* p. 310

SUNDAY BRUNCH WAFFLES

3 ½ cups water

8 oz. (1 cups) tofu

1 Tbs. conc. apple juice

2 ½ cups quick oats

½ cup corn flour or meal

¼ cup cashew nuts*

½ tsp. salt

1. Preheat waffle iron to highest setting.

Hint: Iron may need to be sprayed with Pam for the first waffle, unless you have a new or undamaged teflon iron. One secret for a picture-perfect waffle is to use little or no spray. Too much will make little "holes" on the surface where the drops of spray boil into the batter. Our teflon waffle irons work best when we never spray them! See pictures next page.

2. Blend all ingredients for 1 minute.

Hint: If your blender capacity is less than 6 cups, reserve 11/2 cups of the water to stir in after the mix is blended.

3. Pour mixture onto hot, non-stick waffle iron.

Makes 4 medium waffles

Nutrient Information
Per Serving (¼ waffle)

CALORIES	170
PROTEIN	20%
FAT	30% / 5.5 gm
CARBOHYDRATE	50%
SODIUM	118 mg

Note: The method of pouring the batter onto the iron is ciritcal. Since there is no leavening in this batter, it will not fill out the empty corners of the iron.

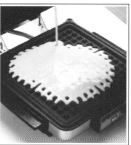

This "pour" would be fine for regular waffles but not here!

Be sure to cover the entire surface with batter...

...and then pour as much more batter onto the whole area as it will hold without running over. This will insure a full two-sided waffle when it is finished baking.

4. Close iron and bake 10 -12 minutes until brown and crisp.

Hint: Remove to a cooling rack and serve. Make several ahead, but make sure they are cool before stacking them. Stacked warm waffles will become soggy and compressed. Toast in oven or toaster just before serving.

Tip: Your waffle should be crisp, light, and golden brown. If your first waffle seems heavy (gummy, with little droplet-sized indentations throughout), add more water to the batter and blend briefly for the second waffle. If waffles are so light and airy they separate, blend in a little more oats into the next batch. Your third waffle is always the best!

Serving tip: New customers at our Sunday Brunch are sometimes skeptical when we suggest they might like a bit of our Non-Dairy Soft Serve on top of a waffle covered with blueberry sauce. But after trying it they almost always come back for seconds! You can do the same thing with Blue- berry Sauce and Blender Ice Cream.

*Throughout the book where nuts are used, they are raw unless indicated otherwise.

2

Our healthy "ice cream*" on those wonderful fruit toppings over waffles makes the whole Sunday Brunch like a dessert!

**See Blender Ice-cream, p. 158*

Filled just right for proper baking but notice the little holes in the upper left. It's the Pam!

Uh oh. There's nothing wrong with the batter, just not enough poured in!

OATMEAL WAFFLES

OATMEAL WAFFLE

3½ cups water

3¼ cups quick oats

¼ cup cashews

2 Tbs. apple juice conc.

½ tsp. salt

Blend and bake according to the instructions in Sunday Brunch Waffles.

Both waffle recipes here are lower in fat than the Sunday Brunch Waffle on page 2 which uses tofu to make a slightly lighter and more tender product as a recipe with eggs might produce. One can actually eliminate the nuts from either of these for an even lower fat version!

BRUNCH WAFFLE #2

3½ cups water

1 Tbs. apple juice conc.

2½ cups quick oats

½ cups corn flour or meal

2 Tbs. cornstarch

½ cup cashew nuts

½ tsp. salt

Variation: Replace 2½ cups quick oats with 1½ cups quick oats and 1¼ cups barley flour. This combination makes a waffle that is light and tender. Try it!

Note: Of all the recipes from the Five Loaves kitchen, I have served waffles on more occasions to more people than any other! I have tried many combinations of flours, grains, beans, and nuts, but I like Sunday Brunch Waffles the best! If you don't have tofu, Brunch Waffle #2 is a close runner-up, especially the variation using barley flour. The cashew nuts in this recipe can be left out for a lower fat version, but they do make it a bit more crisp and light. Whatever you do, don't underestimate the value of the apple juice in this recipe. Without it the waffle will be pale and soft. The apple juice lends crispness and the golden brown color. Even after the hundreds of times I've blended and poured this batter into waffle irons, they aren't always consistent. So don't be too concerned; minor variations, especially at home, aren't a significant problem. These "variations" are likely due to fluctuations in the nutrients and moisture of the grains and flours.

Makes 4 Oatmeal Waffles

Nutrient Information

Per Serving (¼ waffle)

CALORIES	79
PROTEIN	15%
FAT	13% / 1 gm
CARBOHYDRATE	72%
SODIUM	68 mg

Makes 4 Brunch #2 waffles

Nutrient Information

Per Serving (¼ waffle)

CALORIES	96
PROTEIN	12%
FAT	26% / 2.8 gm
CARBOHYDRATE	62%
SODIUM	68 mg

Breakfast—From the Griddle

ORANGE-DATE FRENCH TOAST*

FRUIT TOAST

ORANGE-DATE FRENCH TOAST

½ cup cashews

2 cups water

½ cup date pieces

½ cup orange juice conc.

¾ cup unbleached or whole wheat flour

1 Tbs. vanilla

⅛ tsp. coriander

1. Place all ingredients in blender and *blend for about 2 minutes until smooth.*

2. Pour mixture into a bowl and dip bread one at a time.

   Hint: Bread should not be dripping with batter, so wipe on both sides with another piece of bread or the edge of the bowl.

3. Place bread on a hot non-stick skillet and lightly brown both sides.

   Hint: May be baked in the oven on a non-stick cookie sheet by placing on the bottom rack at 400°. Turn when golden brown on the bottom, and bake a few minutes longer.

*According to Webster's Dictionary, French toast is bread dipped in egg and milk and sautéed. But we have tried many other dips for our bread before "sautéing" and found most of them to work just as well. One idea we've tried when camping is dipping bread in a thin pancake batter and it works great.

SIMPLE FRENCH TOAST VARIATION:

1 cup orange juice (not concentrated)

⅓ cup white flour

6 or 7 slices whole wheat bread

1. Mix flour and juice with wire whip.

2. Dip bread and brown both sides on non-stick skillet.

Serving tip: Use date-nut or raisin bread and serve with almond butter, topped with Apricot or Pear Sauce. Or, for a simple satisfying breakfast, spread French Toast with peanut butter and top with hot applesauce and a bit of pure maple syrup.

FRUIT TOAST

Whole grain toast

Fruit Sauce (p. 6)

Peanut or almond butter (opt.)

Nut milk or soy milk (p. 20)

1. Spread toast with peanut or almond butter (if you like)

2. Place in a wide cereal bowl and top with hot fruit sauce.

3. Pour cold nut or soy milk over and enjoy!

Coats 20 slices of medium sized bread for French Toast
Nutrient Information
Per Serving

CALORIES	262
PROTEIN	10%
FAT	15% / 5 gm
CARBOHYDRATE	75%
SODIUM	300 mg

FRENCH CREPES

MAPLE SYRUP SAUCE

FRESH FRUIT SAUCE

FRENCH CREPES

1 cup quick oats

1 cup whole wheat flour

3 cups water

2 Tbs. raw flax seeds

1 tsp. salt

1 Tbs. apple juice conc. or honey

Variation: Replace flax seeds with ½ cup cashew nuts, or instead of water use soy milk. May use just water and no flax seeds or nuts, but they have a little nicer texture with them.

1. Blend together about 2 minutes until flax seeds are smooth.

2. Pour in ¼ cup portions onto a pre-heated non-stick skillet. Hold pan and tip in a circular motion as you pour so it will flow into a large, thin crepe. Cook on medium-high temperature until dry on top (about 1 min.), then loosen gently with metal spatula and flip over, cooking the other side

for about 30 seconds. Place on a flat plate and stack finished crepes, covering with a cloth to keep warm. May be made a day ahead and refrigerated, wrapping stacked crepes in plastic. Warm in microwave before serving.

Serving Tip: Place a thin layer of sugerless jam on crepe and then spread across the middle a spoon-ful of Whipped Topping (p. 156). Roll up and drizzle with Maple Syrup Sauce or Fruit Juice Maple Syrup

MAPLE SYRUP SAUCE

We dilute pure maple syrup 50/50 with water, bring to a boil and thicken with a small amount of cornstarch.

1 cup pure Maple Syrup

1 cup water

1 Tbs. cornstarch dissolved in ¼ cup water

1. Place Syrup or juice and water in a saucepan and bring to a boil.

2. Slowly stir in the dissolved cornstarch and remove from heat.

3. Serve over crepes, waffles or pancakes.

FRESH FRUIT SAUCE

1 peeled, quartered orange

1 quartered, cored apple

1 banana

1 dash salt

1 tsp. vanilla

1. Blend orange to juice stage. Add the rest of the ingredients and blend until creamy.

2. Serve over waffles, pancakes or toast.

FRUIT JUICE MAPLE SYRUP

1 cup apple juice conc.

2 cups water

1 tsp. maple flavoring

2 Tbs. cornstarch dissolved in ½ cup water

¼ cup sucanat, opt.

Directions same as for Maple Syrup Sauce

Makes 15 French Crepes

Nutrient Information
Per Serving (1 crepe)

CALORIES	79
PROTEIN	14%
FAT	4% / 1 gm
CARBOHYDRATE	82%
SODIUM	40 mg

Makes 3 cups

Nutrient Information
Per Serving (1 cup)

CALORIES	80
PROTEIN	3%
FAT	4% / .4 gm
CARBOHYDRATE	93%
SODIUM	97 mg

Breakfast—From the Griddle

FRUIT SAUCES

APRICOT SAUCE

1 quart canned fruit-juice-sweetened apricots, diced (blend 2 seconds—just to chop)

1 - 12 oz. can frozen conc. apple juice

1 cup crushed pineapple (opt.)

1/4 tsp. almond extract

1/3 cup cornstarch dissolved in 1/2 cup water

CHERRY SAUCE

1 quart canned red, pitted cherries with liquid, unsweetened

2 - 12 oz. cans frozen conc. apple juice

3/8 cup cornstarch dissolved in 1 cup water

1/4 tsp. almond extract

BLUEBERRY SAUCE

5 cups frozen blueberries

1 cup frozen blackberries or Marion berries (opt.)

1 - 16 oz. can frozen conc. apple juice

2 cups water

3/8 cup cornstarch dissolved in 1/2 cup water

PEAR SAUCE

1 quart canned pears, diced

12 oz. can apple juice conc.

1 cup water

2 Tbs. orange juice conc.

1/4 tsp. almond ext.

1/2 Tbs. finely grated orange rind

1/4 cup cornstarch dissolved in 1/2 cup water

1. Place all Fruit Sauce ingredients in a kettle except the dissolved cornstarch.

2. Place over high heat until just beginning to boil. Remove from heat. Be careful not to overcook, especially with blueberries.

3. Slowly stir in the dissolved cornstarch until it thickens.

Hint: Be sure to add the cornstarch slowly and stir briskly to prevent lumps from forming. As you add and stir, it will immediately thicken because it is boiling hot. You can stop adding if it is as you want it, or add more than the recipe calls for if you like it thicker.

4. Return to heat and stir until it just starts to boil. Remove from heat and serve hot or cold over Waffles, French Toast, or toast.

BANANA SAUCE
(see directions below)

2 1/2 cups chilled cashew or soy milk

3 Tbs. fruit juice sweetener or honey

1 Tbs. lemon juice

1 tsp. vanilla

1 tsp. coconut flavoring

4-5 Tbs. Instant Clear Jel, approx.

2 mashed bananas

1. Place all ingredients except bananas and Clear Jel in blender and while blending add Clear Jel a little at a time until milk becomes a thick sauce.

2. Pour into a bowl with mashed bananas and stir. Serve within an hour or the bananas will darken.

This is a great topping to use in the place of whipping cream or ice cream with a fruit topping. If you don't have Clear Jel, you can do this another way, but the first step will have to be done far enough ahead to allow the sauce to cool. Use 1/4 cup cornstarch instead of Clear Jel and place it in a sauce pan. Stir in 1/2 cup of the milk until dissolved. Add all remaining milk and ingredients except mashed bananas (omit Clear Jel). Stir while bringing to a boil, then chill. Whip chilled, thickened milk with a wire whip. Fold in the mashed bananas and serve.

Typical for all fruit sauces
Makes 5 - 7 cups
Nutrient Information

Per Serving (1/2 cup)

CALORIES	98
PROTEIN	2%
FAT	2% / .2 gm
CARBOHYDRATE	96%
SODIUM	13 mg

Strawberry Crepes don't get much better than this! They're made without added fat and are among several kinds you can make at home just as we do at Five Loaves.

Breakfast—From the Griddle

TENDER CREPES

TENDER CREPES

8 oz. tofu

3 cups water

2 cups brown rice flour

¼ cup raw cashews

1 Tbs. apple juice conc.

½ tsp. salt

1. Blend all ingredients in blender until smooth.

2. Pour ¼ cup portions onto a pre-heated non-stick griddle. Or pour in 1 cup portions for large crepes, spreading the batter into a 10 inch circle with the bottom of the dipper.

Hint: Although you may think the batter is too thick for crepes, don't be tempted to thin it with more water, because the result will be gummy crepes that won't cook through.

3. Cook until well browned on the bottom and dry on the top.

Hint: Slip a spatula around the sides to loosen, and then slip under to turn. Make several ahead and keep warm in the oven before serving so they won't disappear faster than they can be made.

APPLE CREPES

Serving Tip: There are many ways to serve this version of the crepe. Tender and delightful, we make hundreds of them every Sunday and present here three of our favorite fillings—Apple, Strawberry and Spinach-Tahini Cheese.

APPLE CREPES

1. Make Crepes and Apple Filling (see next page).

2. Place a generous spoonful of Apple Filling in each crepe and roll up. Place in a serving dish, and top with hot Currant Sauce. Warm in microwave or oven before serving.

STRAWBERRY TORTE

Make five 10-inch crepes and layer them on a platter with Strawberry Filling (see next page) between each layer. Slice into wedges like a pie and serve with Whipped Topping (p. 156).

Makes 16 5″ crepes

Nutrient Information

Per Serving (4 crepes)

CALORIES	292
PROTEIN	22%
FAT	34% / 12 gm
CARBOHYDRATE	44%
SODIUM	278 mg

PANCAKES

PANCAKES

2 cups whole wheat pastry flour

1 tsp. salt

2 cups soymilk or nutmilk

2 Tbs. honey

2 Tbs. Ener-G baking powder (or 1 Tbs. regular baking powder)

1. Blend all together in a blender or with a wire whip. Let sit 5 minutes to become foamy.

2. Pour onto hot griddle, being careful not to stir down the bubbles. Bake until golden brown on each side.

Variation: Add 1 mashed banana or 1 cup blueberries. Other flours may be used instead of whole wheat such as rice, barley, corn, or oat flour.

Makes 8-10 pancakes.

Makes 8 - 10 pancakes

Nutrient Information

Per Serving

CALORIES	109
PROTEIN	13%
FAT	24% / 3.1 gm
CARBOHYDRATE	63%
SODIUM	90 mg

Breakfast—From the Griddle

APPLE FILLING

CURRANT SAUCE

APPLE FILLING

5 cups sliced, golden delicious apples (skins may be left on)

1 - 12 oz. can frozen apple juice conc.

¼ tsp. coriander

½ tsp. cardamom

2 Tbs. cornstarch

½ cup water

1. Place apples and juice in kettle with coriander and cardamom and bring to a boil. Simmer 5 minutes.

2. Dissolve cornstarch in water and stir into apples after they are finished cooking. Simmer 1 minute.

> Hint: Be sure to stir the apples briskly and pour the cornstarch water in slowly to keep lumps from forming. The advantage of stirring in the cornstarch after the fruit has come to a boil is to free you from standing over the stove stirring the whole time the apples are heating and cooking.

Makes 6 cups of filling

Nutrient Information
Per Serving (3/4 cup)

CALORIES	127
PROTEIN	1%
FAT	3% / .4 gm
CARBOHYDRATE	96%
SODIUM	13 mg

For an extra special presentation, make Currant Sauce and spoon over the Apple Crepes.

CURRANT SAUCE

½ cup frozen conc. apple juice

1 cup water

⅛ tsp. each coriander, cardamom, and anise

¾ cup currants or 1 cup raisins

1 Tbs. cornstarch dissolved in ⅛ cup water

1. Place all except cornstarch in a sauce pan and bring to a boil.

2. Stir in dissolved cornstarch and simmer 1 more minute. Remove from heat and serve over Apple Crepes.

> Hint: A tasty alternate in place of currants is to blend raisins with the water, juice, and remaining ingredients until smooth. Cook until thick.

10 />

Breakfast—From the Griddle

STRAWBERRY FILLING

SPINACH FILLING

STRAWBERRY FILLING

2 cups conc. apple juice

¼ cup conc. fruit sweetener or honey

1 cup whole strawberries (if using frozen, thaw completely)

1 quart fresh strawberries, sliced

¼ cup Clear Jel or cornstarch

1. Place juices and whole berries in the blender.

2. Turn on and while blending add ¼ cup Clear Jel until pudding consistency. If using cornstarch, bring blended mixture to a boil in a saucepan, stirring often. Remove from heat and cool for about an hour in the refrigerator.

3. Fold thickened juice into the sliced strawberries.

4. Place one 10 inch crepe on a large platter and cover with 1 cup of berries. Place a second crepe on top and another cup of berries. Repeat layers ending with a generous topping of glazed strawberries and Whipped Topping (p. 156). Slice in 8 pie-shaped wedges to serve.

CHEESY SPINACH FILLING

10 oz. pkg. chopped spinach, drained

½ cup Tahini Cheese (p. 105)

½ cup canned mushrooms (opt.)

1 Tbs. dried onion flakes boiled in ¼ cup water

1 tsp. McKay's Chicken Seasoning

½ tsp. garlic powder

½ Tbs. Liquid Aminos or unfermented soy sauce

Chopped green onions

1. Mix all together and place a heaping tablespoon in each crepe.

2. Roll up and place in a shallow baking dish.

3. Cover and place in 350° oven to warm for 20 minutes.

> *Hint: The microwave works very well for heating these. If this method is used, place in a shallow microwave casserole dish, garnish with Tahini Cheese and green onions, and warm for about 2 minutes before serving.*

4. Remove cover and spoon a small amount of Tahini Cheese down the top center of the crepes and garnish with chives or sliced green onions.

CREAMY SPINACH FILLING

1 cup firm tofu

⅓ cup raw cashew nuts

½ cup water

1 Tbs. lemon juice

1 Tbs. honey

1 Tbs. Imitation Chicken Seasoning

1 Tbs. onion powder

½ tsp. garlic powder

2 tsp. salt

1 Tbs. potato flour

1. Blend together until smooth all the above ingredients.

2. Fold in the following:

1 cup diced red bell pepper

1 can water chestnuts, chopped

1-10 oz. pkg. chopped spinach, cooked and drained

SCRAMBLED TOFU

TOFU SEASONING

SCRAMBLED TOFU

1 - 16 oz. brick firm tofu (2 cups)

3 Tbs. Tofu Seasoning

1 Tbs. Bragg's Liquid Aminos (or 2 tsp. soy sauce)

2 Tbs. canned mushrooms (opt.)

2 Tbs. sliced black olives (opt.)

¼ cup sliced green onions (opt.)

Makes 4 cups

Nutrient Information
Per Serving (½ cup)

CALORIES 95
PROTEIN 38%
FAT 48% / 6 gm
CARBOHYDRATE 14%
SODIUM 167 mg
CHOLESTEROL 0 mg

Note: This is a high fat dish among vegetarian items and should be eaten with this in mind (sparingly!). Notice, for comparison, the figures for "real" scrambled eggs:

Per Serving (one serving at McDonald's)

CALORIES 180
PROTEIN 26%
FAT 70% / 13 gm
CARBOHYDRATE 4%
SODIUM 205 mg
CHOLESTEROL 514 mg!

As you know, there is no cholesterol in ANY plant food. We only included it here since it is such a significant item in eggs. The contrast with the zero amount in tofu is rather enlightening and an encouragement for us to eat more whole plant foods!

1. Add all the seasonings to the tofu and mash with a potato masher.

2. Place in a hot non-stick skillet and cook until done.

   Hint: Use medium-high heat and leave alone until beginning to brown very lightly on the bottom; turn and cook until most of the excess moisture is evaporated and the tofu is beginning to brown lightly on the edges.

3. Add onions, mushrooms, or olives if desired. Serve hot.

TOFU SEASONING

½ cup McKay's Chicken Seasoning

1¼ cups food yeast flakes

¼ cup garlic powder

¾ cup onion powder

¾ tsp. turmeric

Mix together and store in an air-tight container.

OMELETS

TOFU OMELET

16 oz. brick firm tofu

⅓ cup water (omit if using soft tofu)

2 Tbs. Tofu Seasoning (p. 12)

1 Tbs. Bragg's Liquid Aminos or ½ Tbs. soy sauce

2 Tbs. corn flour

2 Tbs. cornstarch

1. Place all in blender and blend smooth.

2. Pour ⅓ cup onto a pre-heated non-stick skillet and spread evenly into a 5 inch circle. Cook until bottom is beginning to brown, and top is dry.

3. Place omelet (see below) filling on half and drizzle a little Tahini Cheese on top of vegetables if desired. Fold the other half of the omelet over the vegetables and let cook for 1 minute.

4. Remove and serve.

OMELET FILLING

1 medium-small zucchini, diced small

1 cup chopped onion

½ cup chopped green or red pepper

¾ cup sliced, pitted olives (green or black)

¾ cup sliced canned mushrooms (use more if fresh)

1 tsp. Vege-Sal or ½ tsp. salt

½ tsp. Italian seasoning

¼ cup water

Simmer together for a brief time on the stove or in Microwave, until vegetables just become tender.

MEXICAN OMELET

1. Follow first two steps of the Tofu Omelet recipe and place a spoonful of Refried Beans (p. 38) in the center of the omelet instead of vegetables. Fold both sides toward the center and let cook for 1 minute.

2. Remove to a platter and drizzle with salsa and Tahini Cheese. Garnish with sliced olives.

BAKED OMELET

1. Make a double recipe of Tofu Omelet

2. Pour half the mixture into a lightly oiled 9 x 13 inch baking dish.

3. Layer with filling of your choice. It can be Mexican, using refried beans and salsa, or vegetable using the omelet filling, or just scatter with mushrooms, peppers, and onions.

4. Pour the rest of the tofu mixture over the filling to cover the top. Drizzle with Tahini Cheese if desired, and garnish with green onions, red peppers, sliced olives, or paprika and parsley or chives.

5. Bake at 350° for 30 - 40 minutes, or until the tofu sets up and is firm.

6. Cut in squares and serve.

Makes 8 Tofu Omelets

Nutrient Information
Per Serving (1 omelet)

CALORIES	334
PROTEIN	40%
FAT	45% / 19 gm
CARBOHYDRATE	15%
SODIUM	496 mg

POTATO PATTIES

HASH BROWNS

POTATO PATTIES

1 cup cashews

1½ cup water

¼ cup McKay's Chicken Seasoning

½ tsp. garlic powder

1 Tbs. onion powder

2 Tbs. potato flour

1 Tbs. dried parsley flakes

1 medium onion, diced small

2 ½ lbs. shredded, cooked potatoes

May be purchased frozen potatoes, but check the ingredients to be sure they are free of hydrogenated oils. If you make them from home cooked potatoes, it works best if potatoes are slightly under-cooked.

1. Blend cashews with all ingredients except potatoes and onions and parsley flakes for at least 1 minute until smooth.

2. Pour over potatoes and onions. Add parsley flakes and mix well with hands.

3. Form patties on sprayed cookie sheet.

Hint: The best method is to pack mix into a ½ cup ice cream scoop and place on cookie sheet. Then flatten them with a spatula, but not too thin.

Gently groom each patty with fingers, pushing the stray potato pieces into a circle.

4. Bake at 400° for 20 - 30 minutes until browned.

Potato Patties are probably the item on our buffet that most people come back for second and third helpings. Crispy brown on the outside, and tender and savory on the inside, many customers say they are just like Latkes, a traditional Jewish favorite.

5. Serve hot with Tofu Sour Cream or Ketchup, or they are very good served plain!

Hint: Leftover patties make great casseroles. Layer with Cream Sauce and precooked onion rings. Or sliced fresh tomatoes, pre-cooked onion rings, and Tahini Cheese diluted half and half with water. Bake until heated through and serve.

HASH BROWNS

This same recipe makes very tasty golden hash-browns. Leav out the potato flour in the blended mix. Instead of forming mix into patties, place a thin layer on a cookie sheet and bake until golden brown on the edges—don't over bake or they will be dry.

Makes 24 patties

Nutrient Information

Per Serving (2 patties)

CALORIES	232
PROTEIN	10%
FAT	23% / 6.5 gm
CARBOHYDRATE	67%
SODIUM	577 mg

Breakfast—Cereals and Milk

OLD FASHIONED BREAD PUDDING

OLD FASHIONED BREAD PUDDING

As far as we know, bread pudding originated in the 1800's in England where it was eaten by the poor to make use of stale bread. Today, we dry the bread on purpose and think of bread pudding as a rich treat.

6 cups dry bread cubes *

½ cup coarsely chopped walnuts

1 cup raisins or currants

1 cup diced apples

4 cups nut or soy milk

¼ cup honey

2 tsp. vanilla

¼ tsp. salt

1 tsp. coriander

1 tsp. grated orange rind (opt.)

⅛ tsp. anise (opt.)

1. Place bread cubes in a mixing bowl along with walnuts, raisins, and apples.

2. Mix remaining ingredients together in a separate container and then add to the bread mixture, stirring lightly until well mixed.

3. Pour into an 8 x 8 inch non-stick or lightly oiled baking dish. Bake at 350° for about 45 minutes. Serve hot.

Prep. time: 15 min.
Baking time: 45 min.

*Sliced bread can easily be cut into ½" cubes and dried in a 250° oven for one or two hours. It is important to dry the bread so that it can absorb more of the flavors of the pudding. You can use any kind of bread that you choose, even muffins or cornbread, but know that the final product will vary greatly depending on the texture and flavor of the bread used.

NO-FAIL OATMEAL CEREAL

NO-FAIL OATMEAL CEREAL

2 cup old fashioned oatmeal

4 cups water

½ tsp. salt

1 cup date pieces

1 cup raisins

1. Place all in a kettle and bring to a boil.

2. Cover with lid and remove from heat. Let stand for 15 minutes. Serve hot.

3. If you add raisins or other dried fruit (please do!), put them in at the beginning and they will soften up just the right amount.

Many cooks wish they knew how to prepare cooked oatmeal in a way that is appealing and appetizing. That's why we're including a recipe here for something so basic. This offers hope for you to change a negative attitude that might exist in your family toward oatmeal mush to a positive one. It is very simple—just don't overcook! The secret is to let the steam slowly do its work so the "mush" (what a name for such a good food!) doesn't become gummy. Then, too, a few diced dates, raisins, or other dried fruits will be sure to delight all who try it.

Makes 8 servings

Nutrient Information
Per Serving

CALORIES	371
PROTEIN	8%
FAT	21% / 10 gm
CARBOHYDRATE	71%
SODIUM	276 mg

Makes 4 cups

Nutrient Information
Per Serving (1 cup)

CALORIES	304
PROTEIN	7%
FAT	5% / 1.5 gm
CARBOHYDRATE	88%
SODIUM	273 mg

ON MAKING GRANOLA

You can make perfect granola every time if you will just watch two critical areas:

MIXING & BAKING

1. Mixing—here is where most beginners make a mistake, but if you catch this simple point, you will have no problem. Just be sure to mix the oats thoroughly with the blended mixture. To do that, simply keep tossing it gently with your hands until all the oats look moist (light brown colored) and there are no dry (whitish colored) oat flakes scattered throughout the mix. Avoid the temptation to squeeze or knead the mix with your hands. You want to retain the shape of the oat flakes without pulverizing them. The properly mixed, finished product will be tender and golden brown, with crispy chunks of various sizes that can be easily broken apart or chewed.

2. Baking—This needs to be baked slowly. If it is baked at too hot a temperature, it will be browned or burned on top, and uncooked underneath. When the uncooked part dries out, it will be tough and hard. Longer, slower cooking is so simple and takes very little attention. Simply bake for about 6 hours and then mix or break up the granola before the last four hours. Or if you prefer larger chunks, turn gently with a large spatula. If you want an even more tender and crispy result, after 8 to 10 hours of baking, turn the oven off leaving the granola for a few more hours.

Hint: A convection oven is the best way to bake granola because of the very even circulation of air, but it is not essential.

NOTE: If oil is used in granola, you can mix it almost any way you want and it will turn out just fine, but this no-oil version is well worth the effort. Most granola at the "store" has enough fat and sugar to essentially be a cookie! But this healthful version will be beautiful if you follow the method given here.

BY THE WAY.

A bowl of granola with raisins, banana slices, and nut milk is a great way to start any day. With a slice or two of toast with millet butter or fruit spread and some other fresh fruit in season, you will be satisfied and energized for a whole morning of activity with no desire for any between meal snacks. If you are not used to this it may take time to accustom your body to being ready for that much food in the morning. One way to increase your morning appetite is to try the two-meal-a-day plan, eating your second meal no later than 3 or 4 o'clock p.m. If this isn't possible for you, try eating a dinner-type meal at noon and only a light supper of fruit and toast. When your body adjusts to this routine, you will sleep so much better and feel so good when you wake up that you'll never want to go back to your old habit of late-night eating!

MAPLE NUT GRANOLA

BANANA GRANOLA

MAPLE NUT GRANOLA

2 cups pitted or chopped dates

½ cup walnuts, roasted peanuts, or almonds

2 Tbs. sesame Tahini (opt.)

1¼ cups hot water

¼ cup honey

1 Tbs. vanilla

1 Tbs. molasses (opt.)

1 tsp. maple flavoring

¾ tsp. salt

12 cups old fashioned rolled oats *(Preferably Quaker or 3 Minute brand—avoid other and most bulk brands—they go to pieces and don't make a tender, flaky granola)*

½ cup coconut (shredded, unsweetened)

1 cup slivered almonds, coarsely chopped walnuts, or roasted peanuts

1. Place dates and ½ cup nuts in blender. Add hot water, honey, vanilla, molasses, maple flavoring and salt. Blend for about 1 minute until smooth.

2. While blending, place the oats, coconut, and nuts in large mixing bowl.

3. Add blended mix to the oats in the large bowl and gently mix together with your hands.

> *Note: Work the wet and dry mixtures together for several minutes until all the oats are all very evenly moistened and coated.*

4. Place in large cake pans or cookie sheets, taking care not to pack or pat it down tightly. Keep it light and airy.

5. Place pans in oven at 200° for about 8 - 10 hours.

> *Hint: It is a good idea to use an oven thermometer to be sure your oven is really 200°. We have found that ovens vary greatly and granola can very easily burn if the temperature is too high. For really tender granola use a convection oven!*

BANANA GRANOLA

½ cup water

1 cup pitted dates

1 tsp. salt

½ tsp. maple flavoring

½ tsp. vanilla

2 large bananas

8 cups rolled oats

1. Blend all ingredients except oats.

2. Pour blended 'sauce' over rolled oats. Mix well. Spread ½ inch thick in untreated baking pan. Bake overnight in 200° oven.

Makes 24 - 1 cup servings

Nutrient Information
Per Serving
CALORIES	130
PROTEIN	8%
FAT	6% / .9 gm
CARBOHYDRATE	86%
SODIUM	134 mg

Makes 10 cups

Nutrient Information
Per Serving (½ cup)
CALORIES	165
PROTEIN	13%
FAT	12% / 2 gm
CARBOHYDRATE	75%
SODIUM	2 mg

MUESLI

POLENTA

MUESLI

1½ cup old fashioned oatmeal

1 cup pineapple juice*

¾ cup canned coconut milk*

1 banana

2 Tbs. honey

½ tsp. salt

1 cup raisins

4 cups diced fresh fruits (apples, peaches, berries, grapes, bananas, pears, or oranges)

1 cup raw or toasted nut pieces (almonds, cashews, or walnuts)

*or use 1¾ cup Piña Colada juice instead

1. Dextrinize oats by placing them in a dry pan over medium-high heat and stirring until just beginning to lightly brown.

2. Blend pineapple juice, coconut milk, banana, honey, and salt until smooth. Add to oats and let sit overnight in refrigerator.

3. In the morning add as desired: raisins, sliced bananas, slivered almonds, coconut, sliced peaches, apples, grapes, berries or other fruits. Serve cold or room temperature.

Muesli is a favorite Scandinavian breakfast which usually consists of raw oatmeal soaked for several hours or overnight, folded into fruit, and garnished with nuts. But grains need to be cooked for the best utilization of the nutrients, so in this recipe we recommend toasting the oats first before soaking it overnight. This not only improves nutrition, but adds a nutty flavor to the dish. Just take care not to toast the oatmeal too long—it can smell and taste burned before it really appears burned.

POLENTA

2 cups cornmeal

6 cups water

2 Tbs. honey

1 tsp. salt

1. Bring all ingredients to a boil while stirring.

2. Pour into 1 large or 2 small bread pans that have been sprayed with Pam and cover with foil. Place in a pan of water in the oven and bake for 1 hour.

3. Remove and chill several hours or overnight.

4. Slice ½-inch thick and brown on both sides on a non-stick griddle, or place on a cookie sheet and bake in a hot oven until just starting to brown—don't let them get too dry.

5. Serve hot with Millet Butter and pure maple syrup, pear sauce, or applesauce.

Makes 8 - 10 servings

Nutrient Information
Per Serving (about 3/4 cup)
CALORIES	341
PROTEIN	2%
FAT	36% / 13.7 gm
CARBOHYDRATE	62%
SODIUM	141 mg

Makes 16 slices

Nutrient Information
Per Serving (1 slices)
CALORIES	124
PROTEIN	9%
FAT	8% / 2 gm
CARBOHYDRATE	83%
SODIUM	267 mg

SOY MILK

SOY MILK
(HOME-MADE)

⅓ cup dry soy beans

2 cups water

6 dates

¼ tsp. salt

¼ tsp. vanilla

2 drops coconut flavoring, optional

4 cups water

1. Cover dry soybeans with plenty of water and let soak for 8 - 12 hours.

2. Drain and rinse soaked soybeans; place in a kettle and cover with water. Bring to a boil and simmer for 10 minutes.

3. Drain and rinse the boiled soybeans; again cover with water, bring to a boil and simmer 10 more minutes.

4. Drain and rinse again. Now beans are ready to blend into milk. I prepare a large amount of beans this way and then freeze them in 1 cup quantities to be thawed and blended into milk as needed.

Hint: This method of boiling, draining and rinsing two times reduces the strong soy bean taste.

5. Blend 1 cup of beans with remaining ingredients in a blender with enough cold water to keep beans moving; blend for several minutes until smooth. Add remaining water to make 4 - 6 cups of milk depending on how rich you prefer the final product.

Optional: Strain through cheesecloth.

6. Chill and serve over cereal of your choice or use in cooking.

⅓ cup dry beans = 1 cup soaked beans

1 pound = 2 cups dry beans

2 cups dry beans = 6 cups soaked beans

6 cups soaked beans yields 9 quarts of milk (1 ¼ gallons)

Makes 6 cups

Nutrient Information
Per Serving (1 cup)

CALORIES	47
PROTEIN	32%
FAT	40% / 2 gm
CARBOHYDRATE	28%
SODIUM	98 mg

Breakfast—Cereals and Milk

CASHEW MILK

ALMOND MILK

CASHEW MILK

1 cup raw cashews

1½ cups water

4 dates or ¼ cup honey

1 tsp. salt

1 tsp. vanilla

5½ cups water

1. Bring cashews and 1½ cups water to a boil.

Hint: This has two purposes, both of which are not absolutely necessary. One is that the cashew milks and creams will keep longer if one "purifies" them with this boiling—it will extend the life of your milk 5 or 6 days.

The second reason is that the "hot" cashews tend to blend a little more easily taking less time to get the same "smooth" result.

Almond: Makes 8 cups

Nutrient Information
Per Serving (½ cup)

CALORIES	65
PROTEIN	4%
FAT	53% / 4 gm
CARBOHYDRATE	43%
SODIUM	134 mg

Cashew: Makes 8 cups

Nutrient Information
Per Serving (½ cup)

CALORIES	64
PROTEIN	10%
FAT	51% / 4 gm
CARBOHYDRATE	39%

2. Drain and rinse boiled cashews and blend with 1½ cups water, dates, salt and vanilla in blender for about 2 minutes until very smooth.

Hint: You may wish to omit the dates or honey and vanilla for milk in cream sauces, soups or gravies.

3. Pour into a pitcher and add 5½ cups more water. Chill.

ALMOND MILK

1 cup raw almonds

2½ cup water

¼ fruit sweetener or honey

1 tsp. salt

1 tsp. vanilla

4½ cups water

1. Bring almonds and 2½ cups water to a boil.

Hint: It isn't necessary to skin the almonds before blending; the straining process takes care of that. You can use almond milk without straining—it just won't be as smooth.

2. Place in blender and blend until smooth.

3. Pour into a clean towel which has been placed over a strainer over a bowl. Close up the towel and squeeze all the liquid out with your hands (save pulp for use in cookies, loafs, etc.)

4. Add remaining ingredients to milk and water to total 7 cups of milk.

Hint: Another very delightful tasting milk can be made by blending together ½ cup each of almonds and coconut and making the same as above.

Mother's milk is a rich food, wonderfully suited for an infant to double its birth weight in five months.

But no human needs milk to drink as a beverage once they have teeth—it's just too rich in fat and calories.*

So these "nut milks," which are also fairly rich, are not intended for drinking as a beverage but as "milk" for cooking or for use in small amounts on cereal, in hot drinks, etc. (cont'd next page)

CASHEW-RICE MILK**

⅓ cup cashew nuts

2 Tbs. honey

1½ cups well-cooked rice

⅜ tsp. salt

2 tsp. vanilla

Approximately 6 cups
  water

1. Place cashews and rice in a saucepan or microwave container and cover with water. Bring to a boil.

  Hint: We generally use left-over rice for this, or we keep portions of rice in the freezer for blending. Cold rice doesn't blend very smooth, so it is important to bring it to a boil with the cashews and water for smooth blending.

2. Place hot cashew and rice mixture in the blender with the remaining ingredients except the remaining water. Turn on and blend thick and smooth, adding a little more water as necessary for efficient blending. Blend for at least 1 minute until no graininess can be seen or felt.

3. Add enough more water to make 5 to 7 cups of milk, depending on the richness desired. A thicker cream can be used over desserts, but thinner is more desirable on cereal or as a drink.

  **This can be made thicker by adding less water in step 3 as desired for a very fine non-dairy "cream."*

  Hint: You may use either brown or white rice. We prefer brown for better nutrition, and though the color of the milk is a shade darker, it is hardly noticable.

The question of getting sufficient calcium is usually cited as reason for continuing the use of milk as a beverage past normal weaning age. As a matter of fact, there are a number of wonderful plant sources of calcium—mainly greens but others as well. Use these as often as you used to drink milk and calcium will be more than sufficient. To name several (1 cup unless otherwise specified):

Broccoli (1 spear)	205 mg
Beet greens	164
Dandelion Greens	147
Chard	102
Kale	94
Almonds (1 oz.)	75
Raisins	71
Brussel Sprouts	56
Lima Beans	54
Cabbage	50

For comparison.

Human milk	79
Cow's milk (1 cup)	291

Makes 7 cups

Nutrient Information
Per Serving (½ cup)

CALORIES	51
PROTEIN	8%
FAT	29% / 1.7 gm
CARBOHYDRATE	63%
SODIUM	59 mg

GUIDE FOR COOKING GRAINS

Grain (1 cup dry)	Water (cups)	Cook (min)	Yield (cups)
Amaranth	3	25-30	3
Barley	3	75	3½
Buckwheat	2	15-20	3½
Bulgar wheat	2	15-20	2½
Cornmeal	4	25	3
Cracked Wheat	2	25	2
Millet (cereal)	4	45-60	3
Oat berries	2-3	45-60	3
Rolled Oats	2	15	2
Quick Oats	2	5	2
Quinoa	2	15-20	4
Brown Rice	2	60	3
Triticale berries (soak overnight)	2¼	40	3
Wild Rice	3	60	4
Whole Wheat	3	120	2
Rye Berries	3	120	2

ENTREES

Enchilada Frijoles and Super Soft Tacos

Meat-like entrees that are hearty and savory are needed to satisfy that "meat and potatoes" appetite many of us have acquired. For many years vegetarian cooks have been making "meatloafs" and "steaks" (burger patties) from nuts, grains, and legumes to fill this need. Eggs are a key ingredient to bind them together and to provide flavor. So the question we are often asked is, "What do you use in your burger patties and loafs if you don't use eggs as a binding agent? The answer is simple—various kinds of flour and a bit of extra liquid or blended tofu do the job very nicely as you will see!

PECAN LOAF

½ cup tofu

2 cups water

4 cups soft whole grain bread crumbs

2 cups ground pecans

1 cup chopped onions

1 Tbs. Bragg's Liquid Aminos

1 ½ tsp. salt

2 Tbs. tomato puree

1 tsp. garlic powder

1 Tbs. onion powder

1 tsp. sage

Makes 10 servings

Nutrient Information

Per Serving

CALORIES	301
PROTEIN	11%
FAT	39% / 14 gm
CARBOHYDRATE	50%
SODIUM	494 mg

1. Blend tofu in 1 cup of the water. Place in bowl with remaining cup of water and all the remaining ingredients. Mix together well.

Hint: A food processor will greatly simplify the preparation of this loaf. The bread can easily be made into crumbs several slices at a time, the pecans can be ground, and the onions chopped.

2. Spread evenly onto non-stick or Pam sprayed 9 x 13 inch baking dish. Bake covered at 350° for 45 minutes. Remove cover and bake 15 more minutes to brown.

Note: Pecans give this loaf its rich, meaty taste. Notice, though, that it has a larger concentration of nuts in its ingredients, and could be thought of as a special-occasion main dish to be served along with other lower fat, high carbohydrate dishes. We serve this at our Thanksgiving buffet with Mushroom Gravy and mashed potatoes.

Prep. Time: 30 min.
Cooking time: 1 hr.

TOFU-WALNUT LOAF

1 - 12 oz. brick tofu*

1 cup water

2 cups soft bread crumbs

1 cup finely chopped
walnuts

1 cup Grape Nuts cereal
(opt.)

1 cup cooked millet or rice

¼ cup corn flour

1 cup chopped onion

½ cup chopped celery

2 Tbs. peanut butter

¼ cup soy sauce

½ tsp. salt

¼ tsp. each:
rosemary
oregano
savory
garlic powder

1. Blend water and tofu
in blender.

2. Mix all other ingredients in a separate bowl.
Add blended tofu and
mix well.

*Hint: A food processor is a
great help in making this
loaf. Soft bread can be
made into crumbs very
quickly, then using the
pulse button, chop the nuts
until the size of Grape
Nuts cereal. Next chop the
onions and celery.*

3. Spread into a 9 x 13 inch
non-stick or Pam-sprayed
pan and cover with foil.
Place in a larger baking
pan filled with water
about ½ inch deep.
Place in oven and bake at
350° about 45 minutes.
Remove from pan of
water and remove foil.
Place in oven and bake
for 20 minutes uncovered
to brown.

4. Remove from oven and
let cool for 10 minutes,
then cut in 12 squares.
Serve with gravy.

*Prep. time: 45 min.
Cooking time: 1 hr.*

*In place of tofu, you can
use 1 cup of soybeans
which have been soaked
overnight (measure after
soaking!), then blended in
1 3/4 cups water (and omit
the 1 cup water in the
ingredients).*

"Let the diet reform be progressive. Let the people be taught how to prepare food without the use of milk or butter. Tell them that the time will soon come when there will be no safety in using eggs, milk, cream, or butter, because disease in animals is increasing in proportion to the increase of wickedness among men. The time is near when, because of the iniquity of the fallen race, the whole animal creation will groan under the diseases that curse our earth.

"God will give His people ability and tact to prepare wholesome food without these things. Let our people discard all unwholesome recipes. Let them learn how to live healthfully, teaching to others what they have learned. Let them impart this knowledge... Let them teach the people to preserve the health and increase the strength by avoiding the large amount of cooking that has filled the world with chronic invalids. By precept and example make it plain that the food which God gave Adam... is the best for man's use as he seeks to regain that sinless state."
E. G. White, 1902

Makes 12 servings

Nutrient Information
Per Serving

CALORIES	258
PROTEIN	17%
FAT	35% / 11 gm
CARBOHYDRATE	48%
SODIUM	555 mg

Entrees—Loafs and Patties

CASHEW CARROT LOAF

CASHEW-CARROT LOAF

2 cups cashew nuts, ground

2 cups raw carrots cut in 1 inch pieces

1 medium onion, chopped

1 cup whole wheat bread crumbs

¼ cup yeast flakes

1 Tbs. lemon juice

⅓ cup water or stock from the carrots

½ tsp. garlic powder

1 Tbs. McKay's Chicken Seasoning

1 tsp. sage

1 tsp. salt

1. Cover carrots with water, cook until tender, pour off and save water, then mash the carrots

2. Mix together all the ingredients and place in a non-stick or Pam-sprayed 2 lb. loaf pan, or a non-stick Bundt cake pan.

3. Cover with foil and bake at 350° for 1 hour. Remove foil and bake 10 more minutes.

4. Let stand in the loaf pan for at least 10 minutes before turning out.

Prep. time: 20 min.
Cooking time: 1 hr, 10 min.

Makes 6 servings

Nutrient Information
Per Serving

CALORIES	310
PROTEIN	10%
FAT	49% / 11 gm
CARBOHYDRATE	41%
SODIUM	685 mg

HARDY HASH

HARDY HASH

1 cooked, shredded potato

1 oatburger (p. 52)

1 tsp. chicken style seasoning

1 Tbs. soy milk

1. Brown shredded potato in a non-stick pan.

2. Slice 1 oatburger into strips

3. Add the chicken style seasoning. Stir gently together and heat.

4. Add the soy milk—this helps to brown and soften potato. Serve hot.

Makes 1 serving

Nutrient Information
Per Serving

CALORIES	287
PROTEIN	13%
FAT	8% / 3 gm
CARBOHYDRATE	78%
SODIUM	555 mg

Entrees—Loafs and Patties

BULGUR "MEAT" LOAF

2 cups water

1 large onion, cut in fourths

3 cloves garlic, peeled

2 medium carrots, peeled and cut into several pieces

1 Tbs. sesame tahini

¼ cup Bragg's Liquid Aminos

1 Tbs. salt

1¼ tsp. powdered thyme

½ cup yeast flakes

1½ cups bulgur wheat

1 cup additional water

1 cup roasted and finely ground walnuts*

½ cup gluten flour (or Do-Pep)

½ cup whole wheat flour

*The walnuts can be roasted at 425° for 10 min., stirring occasionally (watch closely to avoid burning). Then grind in a food processor or blender being careful not to over-process them into a paste.

1. Place carrot and onion pieces in blender along with 2 cups water, tahini, and seasonings. Blend about 10 seconds, just enough to finely chop the vegetables.

2. Pour blended vegetables into a medium saucepan with another 1 cup water and the bulgur wheat. Simmer for 5 minutes, or just long enough to absorb the water.

3. Mix the two flours together and then add them to the bulgur along with the ground walnuts. If the flours aren't thoroughly mixed, the gluten flour may create lumps in the loaf.

4. Spoon mixture into an oiled 1-qt. loaf pan and bake, covered at 350° for 1 hr. Remove foil for the last 10 minutes to brown. Cool the loaf in the pan for about 5 minutes and then remove to serve or cool.

Serving Tip: This loaf is delicious served with Mashed Potatoes and Mushroom Gravy.

Prep. time: 30 min.
Baking time: 1 hr.

"Nuts and nut foods are coming largely into use to take the place of flesh meats. With nuts may be combined grains, fruits, and some roots, to make foods that are health-ful and nourishing. Care should be taken, however, not to use too large a propor-tion of nuts. Those who real-ize ill effects from the use of nut foods may find the diffi-culty removed by attending to this precaution. It should be remembered, too, that some nuts are not so whole-some as others. Almonds are preferable to peanuts, but peanuts in limited quanti-ties, used in connection with grains, are nourishing and digestible."

The Ministry of Healing, p. 298

Makes 8 servings

Nutrient Information
Per Serving
CALORIES 291
PROTEIN 13%
FAT 31% / 10 gm
CARBOHYDRATE 56%
SODIUM 534 mg

SPINACH-TOFU BALLS

1-10 oz. pkg. frozen
  chopped spinach

1 cup tofu

¼ cup Do-pep or gluten
  flour

⅛ tsp. ground rosemary

⅛ tsp. thyme

2 tsp. chicken-like seasoning

½ cup soft bread crumbs

⅛ tsp. garlic powder

½ tsp. onion powder

½ tsp. salt

¼ cup dried onion flakes

¼ cup chopped walnuts
  (opt.)

1. Thaw spinach. Strain
and save water in case
more moisture is needed
in mix.

2. Combine seasonings,
bread crumbs, and gluten
flour; mix well.

   *Hint: It is important to
   mix the gluten flour with
   bread crumbs before adding
   to the wet ingredients,
   otherwise the gluten flour
   will clump together if
   moistened in its concentrated
   form.*

3. Add spinach and finely
mashed tofu and mix
with hands. If mix is too
dry, add a bit of the
spinach juice or water.
Form into balls about
the size of walnuts.

   *Hint: Instead of chopped
   spinach, use an equivalent
   amount of shredded,
   steamed, and drained
   zucchini or carrots.
   Very delicious!*

4. Place on a non-stick
cookie sheet and bake for
30-40 minutes at 350°
until lightly browned.

   *Prep. time: 30 min.
   Baking time: 30 - 40 min.*

Makes 24 small balls

Nutrient Information
Per Serving (2 balls)

CALORIES	89
PROTEIN	20%
FAT	33% / 3.6 gm
CARBOHYDRATE	47%
SODIUM	267 mg

TOFU-WALNUT BALLS

2 - 16 oz. bricks tofu

1 cup water

¼ cup Bragg's Liquid
Aminos

4 cups soft bread crumbs

1 cup finely diced onions
(or ½ cup dried onion
flakes)

1½ cup finely chopped
walnuts

1 cup quick oats

1 tsp. sage

½ tsp. garlic powder

1 tsp. onion powder

1 tsp. Vege-Sal

1 tsp. basil

1 Tbs. McKay's Chicken
Seasoning

1. Place bread crumbs,
walnuts, oatmeal, onions
and seasonings in a large
mixing bowl.

*Hint: Make bread crumbs
out of slices of bread in your
blender or food processor.
Next whiz the walnuts into
fine pieces about the size of
coarse meal. If using a food
processor, the onion can be
finely chopped too.*

2. Blend tofu with water
and Liquid Aminos in
blender; add to the bread
crumb mixture in the
bowl and mix well.

*Hint: If your blender has
less than a 6 cup capacity,
you will have to blend in 2
batches.*

3. Place in mounds on a
non-stick or oiled cookie
sheet. Bake at 350° for 30
minutes or until golden
brown on top and bottom.

*Hint: The fastest, neatest
way to make these is with
an ice cream scoop—large,
medium, or small—what-
ever size you like. The mix
should be quite moist—too
wet to make balls with
your hands. The dryness of
your breadcrumbs will
make a difference with
this, but you can add more
water if they seem too dry.
A dry mix makes a heavier,
drier product, whereas a
moist mix results in a
lighter, more moist and
superior product.*

4. Serve with Sweet-Sour
Sauce (p. 100) or Pasta
Sauce (p. 45).

*Hint: We like to place the
balls in a casserole dish and
drizzle with Sweet-Sour
Sauce or Spaghetti Sauce.
Then heat in microwave or
oven just before serving.*

Prep. time: 30 min.
Cooking time: 30 min.

Makes 40 balls

Nutrient Information
Per Serving (1 ball)

CALORIES	123
PROTEIN	20%
FAT	34% / 5.1 gm
CARBOHYDRATE	46%
SODIUM	196 mg

BREAD DRESSING

9 cups toasted whole
  wheat bread cubes

3 stalks celery, chopped fine

1 cup chopped onion

½ tsp. Savorex or similar

1½ Tbs. McKay's
  Chicken Seasoning

½ tsp. each: marjoram,
  savory, thyme, and
  rosemary

1 tsp. sage

1 Tbs. parsley flakes

½ tsp. garlic powder

1½ cups water

1. Simmer onions, celery,
and seasonings in the
water until tender.

2. Place cubed bread in a
large mixing bowl and
toss with the simmered
onions, and seasonings.
If water is not sufficient
barely to moisten the
bread cubes, sprinkle
enough more water over
the mix to do so, but do
not make it mushy.
Cubes should not lose
their shape.

3. Place in one large or
two small bread pans
that have been coated
with a light non-stick
spray. Cover with foil
and place in a pan of
water in a 400° oven for 1
hour. Check in 30 min-
utes and if it seems a bit
dry, sprinkle with water.

*Serving Tip: Good served
with gravy. Place on a
platter surrounded by
baked potatoes or overlapped
slices of Veggie Cutletts. Delicious as a stuffing for but-
ternut, acorn, or sweet
meat squash.*

Makes 8 servings

Nutrient Information
Per Serving (1 cup)
CALORIES   148
PROTEIN   16%
FAT   10% / 1.8 gm
CARBOHYDRATE   74%
SODIUM   324 mg

VEGGIE CUTLETS

**Canned garbanzos may be used: drain the liquid into a measuring cup, and add water to equal 1 ½ cups total liquid.

2 cups soaked soybeans or garbanzos**

2 Tbs. soy sauce or ¼ cup Liquid Aminos

3 Tbs. McKay's Chicken seasoning

2 Tbs. yeast flakes

1 Tbs. onion powder

½ tsp. garlic powder

2 cups gluten flour or Do-pep

1. To soak soybeans or garbanzos, place at least 1 cup dry beans in about 2 cups of water and leave at room temperature for about 12 hrs.

2. Place 2 cups of soaked, drained beans in a blender with 1 ½ cups water and blend.

3. While blending, add seasonings and blend smooth.

4. Pour into a bowl and add the gluten flour. It will become very stiff and the last of the flour should be kneaded in with your hands. Knead for 3-5 minutes. This can be done in an electric bread mixer or by hand. Longer kneading will make a final product that is more chewy and elastic, while less kneading will make a final product that is more spongy and bread-like.

5. Form into 2 oval-shaped loaves and place on an oiled cookie sheet. Bake 30-40 minutes at 350°, or until nicely browned. Cool on a rack. May be frozen.

6. When cool, slice very thin (about ⅛ inch) and simmer in the following broth for 20 minutes:

BROTH

4 cups water

2 Tbs. Bragg's Liquid Aminos

2 Tbs. McKay's Chicken Seasoning or Beef Seasoning (depending on flavor desired)

7. For a slightly thicker broth,* dissolve 1½ Tbs. cornstarch in ¼ cup water and gradually stir into the simmering cutlets.

8. Serve with mashed potatoes or Bread Dressing (p. 30), or make into Creamy Strogonoff (p. 34).

*This makes a richer, more attractive presentation.

Variation (more similar to home-made gluten):

Follow steps 1 - 4, then instead of shaping into loaves and baking, pinch off walnut-sized pieces and stretch each piece with your fingers into disc-shapped patties. Drop patties into boiling broth and simmer for 20 minutes.

These may be breaded and baked as in Breaded Eggplant (p. 54) or use in place of meat in stews or stir fry.

Makes 8 - 10 servings

Nutrient Information
Per Serving (2 slices)

CALORIES	114
PROTEIN	37%
FAT	7% / .9 gm
CARBOHYDRATE	56%
SODIUM	317 mg

Entrees—Beans and Rice

Nothing is quite as satisfying to a hungry appetite as a platter of rice with some savory combination of legumes and vegetables to serve on top. Cuban Black Beans on Rice consistently rates as a top favorite with our customers, and no doubt much of its success has to do with an appealing presentation. This makes a very fine meal to serve family or guests—it's easy, nutritious, and liked by all.

In this same category, we like to include some of our Mexican favorites. Super Soft Tacos remain an all-time favorite. You might notice that they are lacking in spicy chilies and peppers, but allow yourself to become accustomed to the rich flavors of the beans and sauces without the burning sensation of these hot spices, and you will find that your taste buds enjoy the rich flavors even more!

"Spices at first irritate the tender coating of the stomach, but finally destroy the natural sensitiveness of this delicate membrane. The blood becomes fevered, the animal propensities are aroused, while the moral and intellectual powers are weakened, and become servants to the baser passions. The mother should study to set a simple yet nutritious diet before her family." *Counsels on Diet and Foods,* p. 341

CUBAN BLACK BEANS ON RICE

2½ cups black beans

5 cups water

½ cup diced green or red pepper

¼ cup diced dehydrated onions (or 1 chopped fresh onion)

2 Tbs. yeast flakes

1 ½ tsp. cumin

1 ½ tsp. McKay's Chicken seasoning

1 tsp. onion powder

¾ tsp. garlic powder

¾ tsp. sweet basil

2 Tbs. soy sauce

1 Tbs. lemon juice

1 ½ tsp. Vege-Sal or ¾ tsp. salt

1. Sort* black beans and soak in 10 cups water overnight, or bring to a boil, turn off heat, and let sit one hour.

   Hint: To help reduce gastrointestinal distress, drain off water after the beans are finished soaking and add fresh water to 1 inch above the soaked beans.

2. Add remaining ingredients and bring to a boil, then simmer on low heat for about 1½ hours, or until tender. Serve over brown rice and garnish with Tofu Sour Cream, fresh diced tomatoes, toasted almond slivers, and chopped green onions.

   Cooking time: 1 ½ hr.

*Optional, but for the purpose of cleaning. We often find that pouring the beans onto a cookie pan will allow us to "pick out" little bits of material (dirt, tiny stones, etc.).

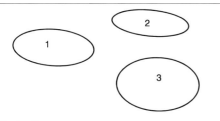

Photo Key:

1. **Long Grain Brown Rice**
2. **A La King Supreme**
3. **Cuban Black Beans on Rice**

Makes 8 cups

Nutrient Information
Per Serving (1 cup)

CALORIES	438
PROTEIN	17%
FAT	5% / 2.7 gm
CARBOHYDRATE	78%
SODIUM	223 mg

Entrees—Beans and Rice

LENTIL STROGANOFF

CREAMY STROGANOFF

LENTIL STROGANOFF

2 cups lentils

3½ cups water

1 med. diced onion or ⅓ cup dried chopped onions

1 tsp. garlic powder

2 tsp. basil

1 tsp. salt

1 Tbs. soy sauce or 1½ Tbs. Bragg's Liquid Aminos

3 Tbs. yeast flakes

1¼ cups water

1 Tbs. tomato paste

5 Tbs. unbleached flour

1. Place lentils and water in a large kettle and simmer for 1 hr.

2. At the end of 1 hr. add diced onions and seasonings. Cook additional 15 minutes.

3. Meanwhile, in a small bowl, mix together the 1¼ cups water, tomato paste and flour.

4. Stir flour and water mixture slowly into the hot lentils and if desired add 1 cup canned mushrooms. Serve over brown rice or pasta.

Prep. time: 20 min.
Cooking time: 1 ½ hr.

CREAMY STROGANOFF

¾ cup cashew nuts

1 cup water

1 cup tofu

2 Tbs. Bragg's Liquid Aminos

2 Tbs. McKay's Beef Seasoning

2 Tbs. onion powder

3 Tbs. yeast flakes

2 cups water

2 cups Veggie Cutlets (p. 31),* cut or torn into pieces

1 onion, sliced into thin strips

1 cup or more canned mushrooms, or 2 cups fresh, sliced mushrooms

2 Tbs. cornstarch dissolved in ¼ cup water

*Canned Gluten pieces such as Worthington Scallops may be used

1. Place cashews and tofu in blender with 1 cup water; blend smooth.

2. While blending add seasonings and then the remaining 2 cups water after it has blended smooth.

3. Meanwhile, saute onions and mushrooms in a small amount of water until tender. Stir in the blended tofu mixture and the gluten pieces. Stir and just bring to a boil, then quickly add dissolved cornstarch and stir as you remove it from the heat. You don't want to boil it very long or the texture may become slightly curdled.

4. Serve over brown rice or pasta.

Makes 8 cups Lentil Stroganoff

Nutrient Information
Per Serving (1 cup lentils on 1 cup rice)

CALORIES	410
PROTEIN	19%
FAT	5% / 2.3 gm
CARBOHYDRATE	76%
SODIUM	412 mg

Makes 8 cups Creamy Stroganoff

Nutrient Information
Per Serving (1 cup Stroganoff on 1 cup rice)

CALORIES	358
PROTEIN	14%
FAT	22% / 9.1 gm
CARBOHYDRATE	64%
SODIUM	657 mg

CALYPSO STEW

COUSCOUS

CALYPSO STEW

2 cups calypso beans*

1 tsp. cumin

1½ tsp. McKay's Chicken Seasoning

1 tsp. Vege-Sal

Salt to taste

1 tsp. basil

½ tsp. paprika

¼ tsp. oregano

1 tsp. dill weed

1 large carrot, sliced or diced

2 cups shredded green cabbage

1 cup shredded red cabbage

1 large onion, cut in long, thin strips

1 cup sliced celery

3 cups canned diced tomatoes in juice

Calypso beans are a black and white bean found in some co-ops. You can substitute pinto, kidney beans, or garbanzos.

1. Soak dry beans overnight or boil in water and let soak one hour. Drain and discard water.

2. Cover soaked beans with water in a large kettle 1 inch above beans (or use 4 cups of canned beans of your choice). Bring to a boil and simmer until nearly done, about 2 hours.

3. Add seasonings and diced carrot; cook for 15 minutes, then add the remaining ingredients and cook 15-20 minutes longer or until vegetables are tender. You may need to add more water to achieve the consistency of a thick stew. Serve over rice or couscous.

Prep. time: 30 min. (plus one hr. soaking time)
Cooking time: 2 ½ hr.

MICROWAVE COUSCOUS

4 cups couscous

4 cups water

½ tsp. salt

1. Place couscous in a shallow, wide microwave container in which it will not be deeper than ½ inch. Cover with water and salt.

2. Microwave uncovered for about 3 minutes. Toss gently with a fork. Microwave 3 more minutes or until done.

Prep. time: 5 min.
Cooking time: 6 min.

Makes 10 cups

Nutrient Information

Per Serving (1 c. stew on 1 c. couscous)

CALORIES	205
PROTEIN	20%
FAT	4% / .96 gm
CARBOHYDRATE	76%
SODIUM	51 mg

A LA KING SUPREME

CREAMED ASPARAGUS

A LA KING SUPREME

¼ cup cashew nuts

⅜ cup unbleached flour (may use spelt or whole wheat)

2 Tbs. tahini (opt.)

1½ tsp. onion powder

1½ tsp. salt

1 Tbs. McKay's Chicken Seasoning

2 Tbs. yeast flakes

½ tsp. garlic powder

1 tsp. basil

4 cups water

1 medium onion, diced

½ cup diced red sweet pepper

½ cup sliced canned mushrooms

1½ cups cooked or canned garbanzo beans

1 cup frozen peas

½ cup water chestnuts (opt.)

1. Place cashews in blender with 2 cups of the water. Add flour and seasonings and blend for about 2 minutes until very smooth.

2. Simmer onion and peppers in a small amount of water for about 8 minutes.

3. Add blended cashew mixture along with the remaining 2 cups of water. Stir while bringing to a boil.

   Hint: If there is some water still left in the onions and peppers after cooking, measure or estimate how much and add that much less than the 2 cups of water.

3. Add garbanzos, peppers, and peas.

   Hint: Just stir in the peas and heat to serving temperature, but don't bring to a boil again. You want the peas to retain their bright green color.

4. Serve over brown rice or quinoa.

*Prep. time: 30 min.
Cooking time: 15 min.*

CREAMED ASPARAGUS

2 cups fresh asparagus, cut in 1 inch pieces (or use frozen asparagus)

1 medium onion

½ cup diced red pepper, or ¼ cup diced pimiento

1 cup sliced mushrooms

A La King Supreme cream sauce (this page)

1. Follow step one of the A La King Supreme recipe to make A La King Supreme cream sauce.

2. Simmer asparagus, mushrooms, and peppers together until tender.

3. Add blended cream sauce along with 2 cups water and bring to a boil. Serve hot over rice or quinoa.

   *Prep. time: 30 min.
   Cooking time: 15 min.*

Makes 8 cups

Nutrient Information

Per Serving (1 c. Ala King on 1 c. rice)

CALORIES	387
PROTEIN	12%
FAT	19% / 8.4 gm
CARBOHYDRATE	69%
SODIUM	481 mg

Makes 8 cups

Nutrient Information

Per Serving (1 cup Asparagus on 1 cup rice)

CALORIES	367
PROTEIN	13%
FAT	21% / 8.6 gm
CARBOHYDRATE	66%
SODIUM	502 mg

Entrees—Beans and Rice

VEGETABLE CURRY

SAVORY QUINOA

VEGETABLE CURRY

2 cups water

2 medium potatoes, pared and diced

1 large carrot, peeled and diced

2 celery sticks, sliced

2 cups fresh or frozen green beans, cut small

1 medium onion, diced

1 - 15 oz. can garbanzos (2 cups) including juice

1 Tbs. grated lemon rind (opt.)

1½ Tbs. lemon juice

1 tsp. salt

2 Tbs. McKay's Chicken Seasoning

1 tsp. cumin

1 tsp. turmeric

1 tsp. coriander

1 tsp. garlic powder

1 cup tofu

2 Tbs. Bragg's Liquid Aminos

¾ cup well cooked rice

⅔ cup cashew nuts

2 cups water

3 Tbs. unbleached flour (or 2 Tbs. cornstarch)

1. Prepare vegetables and place in a large kettle with the 2 cups water and all the seasonings. Cook about 20 minutes, until tender.

2. Meanwhile, dice the tofu and coat with about 2 Tbs. Liquid Aminos and place on a cookie sheet. Bake in oven at 350° for about 20 minutes, until browned and puffy.

3. Blend the cashews and rice in water until smooth, adding the flour while blending.*

4. Add the blended cashew mixture to the cooked vegetables and stir until it begins to boil and thicken. Remove from heat and add the baked tofu cubes.

5. Serve over hot brown rice or quinoa.

*Prep. time: 40 min.
Cooking time: 20 min.*

Vairation: Use 1 - 8 oz. can coconut milk in place of the cashew nuts, rice and water in step #3.

SAVORY QUINOA

2 cups quinoa

4 cups water

1 cup diced green onion (or ¼ cup dried onion flakes)

¼ cup diced red pepper

2 tsp. Bragg's Liquid Aminos (or soy sauce)

1 tsp. cumin

2 tsp. basil

2 tsp. onion powder

½ tsp. garlic powder

2 Tbs. McKay's Chicken Seasoning

2 Tbs. food yeast flakes (opt.)

1 tsp. salt

Place all ingredients in a saucepan or rice cooker. Bring to a boil and simmer 20 minutes or until done. Serve as you would rice.

Serves 6

Vegatable Curry
Makes 10 cups
Nutrient Information
Per Serving (1 cup)

CALORIES	457
PROTEIN	12%
FAT	18% / 9.6 gm
CARBOHYDRATE	70%
SODIUM	816 mg

Entrees—Beans and Rice

SUPER SOFT TACOS

REFRIED BEANS

SUPER SOFT TACOS

1 quart "Refried" Beans
(next column)

12 thin corn tortillas or 6 flour tortillas

1 ½ cups diced tomatoes

1 large avocado

½ cup Tofu Sour Cream
(opt. p. 92)

4 cups finely shredded lettuce

1 cup Tahini Cheese
(p. 105)

1 cup sliced olives

3 cups salsa or Pasta Sauce

1. Warm tortillas in microwave just until soft.

2. Quickly fill each in the following order:

⅓ cup "Refried" Beans
1 Tbs. Tofu Sour Cream
1 avocado slice
2 Tbs. diced tomatoes
⅓ cup shredded lettuce

3. Fold each filled tortilla in half and arrange in a shallow casserole or platter.

4. Pour heated salsa or Pasta Sauce across a large portion of the center of the tacos. Drizzle with Tahini Cheese, and sprinkle with sliced olives. A last finishing touch that looks great is to sprinkle Non-Dairy Parmesan Cheese on top. Serve immediately or warm slightly more in microwave or oven before serving.

Alternate serving tip: Mash avocado with Tofu Sour Cream and serve as Guacamole. Serve all the ingredients in individual dishes and let each person assemble his/her own taco.

Prep. time: 1 hr. (May take less if some ingredients are made ahead)

"REFRIED" BEANS*

5 cups dry pinto beans, covered with water and soaked overnight (or bring to a boil, turn off heat, and soak 1 hr.)

1 Tbs. garlic powder

⅜ cup onion powder

2 Tbs. McKay's Chicken Seasoning (or 2 tsp. salt)

⅜ cup Bernard Jensen's Gravy Seasoning

2 Tbs. cumin

1½ Tbs. basil

1. Drain soaking water off the beans and cover to 1 inch above the top of the beans with fresh water. Cook with remaining ingredients for about 2 hours, until beans are tender.

2. To beans add 1 cup Tahini Cheese and mash well with a potato masher, mixer, or hand blender.

Hint: This is a large recipe for your convenience. Divide into three one quart portions, and freeze two. Each portion should fill 30 tacos, using 2 Tbs. per tortilla. Using 3 tacos per person, one quart should serve 10 people.

Prep. time: 15 min. (not counting soaking time) Cooking time: 2 hr.

*In "Mexican" foods, beans are frequently boiled in fat, often lard, and called "refried." Here is a more healthy alternative—boil in water and use rich seasonings for a result just as good or better!

Makes 12 Tacos

Nutrient Information
Per Serving (1 Taco)

CALORIES	118
PROTEIN	12%
FAT	32% / 4 gm
CARBOHYDRATE	57%
SODIUM	159 mg

Makes 12 cups

Nutrient Information
Per Serving (½ cup)

CALORIES	157
PROTEIN	22%
FAT	4% / .6 gm
CARBOHYDRATE	74%
SODIUM	209 mg

Entrees—Beans and Rice

ENCHILADA FRIJOLES

ENCHILADA SAUCE

ENCHILADA FRIJOLES

3 cups mashed Black
  Beans (p. 31) or
  Refried Beans (p. 36)

16 corn tortillas

3 cups Enchilada Sauce
  (this page)

1⅓ cup Tahini Cheese
  (p. 105)

½ cup each sliced olives
  and diced green onions
  (opt.)

Using a rectangular
9 x 13 inch baking dish,
layer the above
ingredients in the
following order:

*1. Spread 1 cup Enchilada
Sauce in dish*

2. Lay 4 tortillas over sauce

*3. Spread with 1½ cup
layer of beans*

4. 4 more tortillas

5. 1 cup of Enchilada Sauce

*6. Drizzle with ⅔ cup
Tahini Cheese*

7. 4 more tortillas

*8. Spread with 1½ cup
layer of beans*

9. 4 more tortillas

10. 1 cup Enchilada Sauce

Cover and bake 30 min-
utes at 350°. Remove
cover and drizzle with ⅔
cup Tahini Cheese.
Sliced olives and
chopped green onions
may also be added as a
garnish. Serve after it has
cooled for 10 or 15 min-
utes. This will give it
time to firm up and the
cheese to melt.

Prep. time: 30 min.
Cooking time: 30 min.

Makes 8 servings

Nutrient Information
Per Serving

CALORIES	150
PROTEIN	10%
FAT	25% / 4.8 gm
CARBOHYDRATE	65%
SODIUM	402 mg

ENCHILADA SAUCE

1 - 15 oz. can tomatoes

1 - 15 oz. can tomato sauce

½ small can (6 oz.)
  tomato paste

¼ cup honey or fruit
  sweetener

½ tsp. garlic powder

½ tsp. salt

¼ tsp. basil

½ tsp. cumin

¼ cup fresh chopped
  cilantro (opt.)

1 cup diced onion

½ cup diced green pepper

Cook onion and pepper
in ¼ cup water until
tender. Add remaining
ingredients and cook for
½ hour.

Prep. time: 20 min.
Cooking time: 40 min.

Makes 4 cups

Nutrient Information
Per Serving (1 cup)

CALORIES	140
PROTEIN	9%
FAT	5% / .7 gm
CARBOHYDRATE	86%
SODIUM	467 mg

Entrees—Beans and Rice

JAMAICAN RICE

FRIED RICE

JAMAICAN RICE & PEAS

1 cup black-eyed peas

1 cup canned coconut
   milk

1 medium diced onion

1 tsp. salt

1 tsp. thyme

1 tsp. garlic powder

2 tsp. Vege-Sal

6 cups water

2 cups long grain
   brown rice

1. Place peas in a kettle
and add all remaining
ingredients except rice.
Simmer for 1 hour.

2. Add rice and simmer
for 30 minutes. Stir
lightly with a fork and
continue cooking until
rice is tender, about 15
minutes more.

*More water should be added
if it is all absorbed before the
rice is finished cooking.*

3. Serve.

*Cooking time: 1 hr. 45
min.*

Makes 10 servings

Nutrient Information
Per Serving
CALORIES 245
PROTEIN 12%
FAT 22% / 6 gm
CARBOHYDRATE 66%
SODIUM 364 mg

FRIED RICE

1 cup finely chopped onion

1 clove garlic, chopped
   fine

1 cup fresh mushrooms
   or eggplant, chopped

1 cup tofu, mashed

1 ½ Tbs. McKay's
   Chicken Seasoning

1 tsp. marjoram

1 ½ tsp. basil

½ tsp. dill weed

1 tsp. fructose (opt.)

1 Tbs. parsley flakes

1 cup frozen peas

4 cups cooked long grain
   brown rice

*Hint: The rice should be
cooked only until tender,
and refrigerated for a day
or two uncovered to allow
a bit of drying. Freshly
cooked, hot rice is usually
too sticky.*

1. Place tofu in hot
non-stick skillet, adding
½ Tbs. of the McKay's.
Cook and stir now and
then until it has become
well-cooked and almost
tough.

2. Add the chopped
onions and eggplant or
mushrooms and garlic
and continue stir frying
with the heat turned on
med-high for about 4
minutes.

3. Add the rice and
remaining seasonings
(including the remaining
Tbs. McKay's, or less if
the rice was salted when
cooked) and stir only
until the rice is very hot.
The entire process takes
about 10 minutes. Do
not add water as you fry
or the fried rice texture
will be lost.

4. Add peas at the very
last and stir in for a few
seconds until they become
hot and then remove
from heat. Serve with
coarsley chopped roasted
almonds and Bragg's
Liquid Aminos if desired.

*Mexican Fried Rice
Variation:*

*Replace mushrooms or
eggplant with 1 cup diced
red pepper.*

*Replace tofu with 1 cup
black beans, drained and
rinsed.*

*Replace majoram with
1 tsp. cumin.*

*Replace frozen peas with
1 cup corn.*

Makes 6 servings

Nutrient Information
Per Serving
CALORIES 199
PROTEIN 20%
FAT 19% / 4.4 gm
CARBOHYDRATE 61%
SODIUM 296 mg

40

CARROT RICE CASSEROLE

CARROT RICE CASSEROLE

1 medium onion, chopped

½ bell pepper, minced

1 cup water

2 cups cooked rice

2 cups finely grated carrots

1 cup bread crumbs
(takes 4 slices of bread)

4 Tbs. flour

1½ tsp. salt

½ tsp. garlic powder

2 Tbs. yeast flakes

½ cup peanut butter

1. Simmer onion and bell pepper in small amount of water.

2. Combine all ingredients and spoon into a baking dish.

A shallow baking dish is best—ingredients should be about 1 inch deep.

3. Bake at 350° for 45 minutes covered, then remove cover and bake 10 minutes.

Makes 6 servings

Nutrient Information
Per Serving
CALORIES	230
PROTEIN	13%
FAT	43% / 11.5 gm
CARBOHYDRATE	44%
SODIUM	475 mg

Hint: Another quick way to make this is in the blender. Place water and all ingredients except rice in the blender. Carrots can be pared, but not grated—just cut them in several large pieces. The onions can be quartered. Turn on blender for a few seconds until carrots are minced. Fold into the rice and place in the baking dish.

Serving tip: This is especially good served with a topping of Creamed Peas (p. 70), using one 10 oz. pkg. of peas instead of two.

"Grains, fruits, nuts, and vegetables constitute the diet chosen for us by our Creator. These foods, prepared in as simple and natural a manner as possible, are the most healthful and nourishing. They impart a strength, a power of endurance, and a vigor of intellect that are not afforded by a more complex and stimulating diet."

The Ministry of Healing, p. 296

MILLET CASSEROLE

MILLET CASSEROLE

4 cups canned tomatoes

2 Tbs. raw sunflower seeds or ¾ cups cashew nuts

1 onion

1 cup raw millet

1 cup chopped olives, opt.

1 - 2 tsp. salt

2 tsp. Italian seasoning

1. Blend tomatoes, sunflower seeds and onion until smooth.

2. Add the rest of the ingredients and mix well.

3. Place in a casserole dish. Cover and bake for 1½ hours at 350°.

Variation: For a more mild flavored loaf, use 3 cups tomato juice and 2 cups water instead of canned tomatoes.

Makes 8 cups

Nutrient Information
Per Serving (1 cup)
CALORIES	195
PROTEIN	12%
FAT	13% / 3 gm
CARBOHYDRATE	75%
SODIUM	245 - 493 mg

Entrees—Beans and Rice

SAVORY LENTILS

SAVORY RED BEANS

SAVORY LENTILS

2 cups dry lentils

1 - 8 oz. can tomato sauce

4 ½ cups water

1 large onion, chopped

⅛ tsp. cumin

¼ tsp. oregano

3 crushed juniper berries (opt.)

1½ tsp. salt

¼ tsp garlic powder

¼ tsp. basil

¼ tsp. paprika

Wash and drain the lentils. Add all ingredients and cook for 1 hr. If a crock-pot is used, place on automatic for 6 to 8 hours.

Serving Tip: Lentils make a very fine main dish, combined with salads, bread, avocado, or any vegetable and a simple dessert. Try spooning hot lentils over toast that has been spread with Tofu Mayonnaise and avocado slices. Another great serving idea is lentils over baked spaghetti squash.

Makes 4 cups

Nutrient Information
Per Serving (½ cup)

CALORIES	237
PROTEIN	27%
FAT	3% / .8 gm
CARBOHYDRATE	70%
SODIUM	800 mg

SAVORY RED BEANS

4 cups small red beans (pink or pinto may also be used)

1 cup tomato sauce

9 cups water

¼ cup green pepper, diced

2 medium onions, diced

½ tsp. garlic powder

¼ tsp. each: dill, oregano, basil, celery salt, paprika

2 tsp. salt

1. *Crock pot method:* Wash beans well, drain, add all ingredients, and place in pot 18-20 hours. To speed up the cooking time, boil the water first before placing it in the crockpot.

2. *Stove-top method:* Soak beans overnight. Drain off the soaking water and cover with new water and all the ingredients. Cook for 3-4 hours.

Makes 2 quarts

Nutrient Information
Per Serving (¾ cup)

CALORIES	227
PROTEIN	25%
FAT	4% / 1.6 gm
CARBOHYDRATE	71%
SODIUM	728 mg

Entrees—Pasta And Tofu Dishes

Ｗe are happy to share some of our favorite pasta dishes. You will love this Lasagna recipe because it is both simple to make and delicious. A customer recently asked if he could order a whole casserole to take home and freeze for his teen-age son. "He likes it better than the kind people make with cheese and meat and white pasta (we use whole wheat lasagna), and he doesn't have any particular interest in healthful eating—I figure I might as well provide him with a better alternative as long as he likes it."

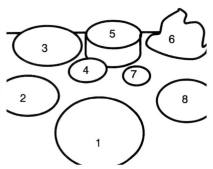

Photo key:
1. **Spinach Manicotti**
2. **Veggie Quiche**
3. **(same as 2)**
4. **Sweet 'n Sour Sauce**
5. **Tofu-Walnut balls on Quinoa**
6. **Five Loaves French Bread**
7. **Millet Butter**
8. **Vegetarian Pizza**

Entrees—Pasta and Tofu Dishes

LASAGNA

TOFU FILLING

LASAGNE

1 recipe Pasta Sauce (p. 45)
or 6 cups spaghetti sauce
(such as Healthy Choice)

1 recipe Tofu Filling (this
page)

12 whole wheat lasagna
noodles

1 cup Tahini Cheese
(p. 105)

Olives

Green onions

Non-dairy Parmesan
Cheese, opt. (p. 104)

1. Lightly coat a 9 x 13
inch casserole dish with
Pam, and ladle 1½ cups
of Pasta Sauce in the
bottom.

2. Place uncooked
noodles length-wise, and
spread 3 cups of tofu
filling on top of noodles.

3. Repeat procedure and
top with a third layer of
noodles and sauce.

4. Cover and bake 1 hr. at
350°. When done remove
covering and drizzle with
Tahini Cheese and gar-
nish with sliced olives,
green onions, and diced
red peppers if desired. Finally, sprinkle with Non-
Dairy Parmesan Cheese.

5. Let stand for about 15
minutes before serving.

*Hint: During this time the
heat from the hot Lasagna
will cause the cheese to
melt and change color,
giving it a baked (but not
over-baked) look. If you
bake it with the cheese on,
it will not look as fresh and
appetizing. Standing also
makes it easier to cut and
serve as it sets up, so, if
possible, plan this extra
time in your baking and
serving schedule. This can
be assembled a day ahead
and baked the next day. It
also freezes very well, but
should be baked first.*

TOFU FILLING

5 cups shredded zucchini
(or 2 - 10 oz. pkgs. frozen,
chopped spinach,
thawed and drained)

3 cups mashed firm tofu

1 small onion, diced

1½ tsp. Italian seasoning

1 tsp. garlic

1 tsp. salt

2 tsp. basil

1½ Tbs. McKay's Chicken
Seasoning

1. Place diced onion and
shredded zucchini in a
saucepan with 2 Tbs.
water and simmer for 5
minutes. If using frozen,
chopped spinach, only
the onion needs to be
pre-cooked, or use ⅓ cup
dried onion flakes.

2. Meanwhile, mash tofu
and add seasonings. Stir
in the zucchini and onion.

Prep. time: 15 min.

Cooking time: 5 min.

Makes approx. 6 cups

TOFU MANICOTTI

*Variation: For Stuffed Mani-
cotti, par-boil 12 manicotti
pasta tubes, for 5 minutes.
Drain and stuff with Tofu
Filling. Cover with Pasta
Sauce (p. 45) and bake.*

Makes 12 servings

Nutrient Information
Per Serving

CALORIES	314
PROTEIN	19%
FAT	27% / 10 gm
CARBOHYDRATE	54%
SODIUM	476 mg

Makes 6 cups

Nutrient Information
Per Serving

CALORIES	78
PROTEIN	34%
FAT	36% / 3.5 gm
CARBOHYDRATE	30%
SODIUM	360 mg

SPAGHETTI & MEATBALLS

PASTA SAUCE

SPAGHETTI & MEATBALLS

2 lb. spelt, soy, or Durham spaghetti cooked according to package directions

1 recipe Pasta Sauce (p. 45)

1 recipe Spinach-Tofu Balls (p. 28), or Tofu Walnut Balls (p. 29)

½ recipe Tahini Cheese, (p. 105) or Parmesan Cheese (p. 104)

To serve, place plain cooked spaghetti on a large platter, or on individual plates, cover with Spaghetti Sauce, place Spinach Tofu Balls on top, and drizzle Tahini Cheese over balls, and/or sprinkle with Non-dairy Parmesan Cheese.

Prep. time: 1 hr. (less if sauces already made)
Cooking time: 15 min.

Variation:
Instead of meat balls and Tahini Cheese, top with Pesto Sauce, p. 101.

PASTA SAUCE

1 - 15 oz. can crushed tomatoes in puree (or tomato puree)

1 - 6 oz. can tomato paste

½ cup pitted olives

3 cups water

¼ cup fruit sweetener or honey

1 Tbs. molasses

1 Tbs. lemon juice

½ Tbs. dried parsley flakes

¼ cup dried onion flakes

1 tsp. salt

1 tsp. basil

½ tsp. Italian seasoning

¾ tsp. garlic powder

2½ Tbs. cornstarch dissolved in ¼ cup water

1. Place crushed tomatoes and tomato paste in a 2-quart or larger kettle.

2. Place olives in the blender with 1½ cups of the water. Blend for at least 1 minute until the olives are pureed as smooth as possible. Add to the tomatoes in the kettle along with the remaining 1½ cups of water.

Hint: The pureed olives give the sauce a richer flavor and texture without the use of refined oils.

3. Add all the remaining ingredients except the cornstarch.

4. Bring to a boil and simmer for at least an hour.

5. Gradually stir in the cornstarch water, stirring briskly to keep from lumping and then remove from heat. It is now ready to serve over spaghetti, or in any recipe such as Lasagna, Manicotti, or Eggplant Parmesan.

Prep. time: 20 min.
Cooking time: 1 hour minimum
(2 hours is better)

Makes 8 servings

Nutrient Information
Per Serving

CALORIES	456
PROTEIN	14%
FAT	15% / 7.6 gm
CARBOHYDRATE	71%
SODIUM	341 mg

Makes 6 cups
Nutrient Information
Per Serving (3/4 cup)

CALORIES	127
PROTEIN	7%
FAT	5% / .8 gm
CARBOHYDRATE	88%
SODIUM	429 mg

Entrees—Pasta and Tofu Dishes

EGGPLANT PARMESAN

PASTA ITALIANA

EGGPLANT PARMESAN

3 medium eggplants

4 cups soft bread crumbs

1 recipe Pasta Sauce (p. 45), or about 5 cups spaghetti sauce of choice

1 recipe Tofu Filling (p. 44), omitting zucchini or spinach

1. Score the skins of the eggplants by slicing through the skin from top to bottom in about 6 places around the eggplant. Slice the eggplant in ¼ inch thick round slabs and place them on non-stick cookie sheets. Bake at 350° until cooked through and beginning to brown a bit.

2. Place 1½ cups Pasta Sauce in the bottom of a 9 x 13 inch glass casserole dish that has been lightly treated with Pam.

3. Arrange baked eggplant slices evenly over the sauce in one layer.

4. Spread 1½ cups Tofu Filling over the eggplant slices.

5. Place 1½ cups of bread crumbs evenly over the Tofu Filling.

6. Repeat steps two through five.

7. Now that you have layered everything twice, finish it off with a final layer of eggplant and sauce.

8. Season the remaining bread crumbs with 1 tsp. salt, 1 Tbs. yeast flakes, and 1 tsp. paprika. Cover the top with seasoned crumbs and dot here and there with any remaining tofu if desired.

9. Cover and bake for 45 minutes at 350°.

10. Remove cover and bake uncovered for 15 minutes until top is lightly browned. Let it cool about 15 minutes before serving to give it time to firm up. Sprinkle top with Non-Dairy Parmesan Cheese if desired.

Prep. time: 60 min.
Cooking time: 60 min.

PASTA ITALIANA

½ pound whole wheat macaroni

2 - 16 oz. cans diced tomatoes

2 - 16 oz. cans red kidney beans, drained

1 cup crushed tomatoes

4 oz. mushrooms, opt.

1 clove garlic, minced

1 bay leaf

1 tsp. onion powder

1 tsp. parsley, chopped

½ tsp. sweet basil

½ tsp. oregano

1. Cook macaroni as directed on the package.

2. Meanwhile, bring remaining ingredients to a boil, then simmer for 20 minutes. Remove bay leaf, and stir into macaroni. May be baked as a casserole, or served immediately.

Variation: Substitute cooked brown rice for macaroni.

Makes 10 - 12 servings

Nutrient Information
Per Serving

CALORIES	195
PROTEIN	12%
FAT	14% / 3 gm
CARBOHYDRATE	74%
SODIUM	288 mg

Makes 10 servings

Nutrient Information
Per Serving (1 cup)

CALORIES	192
PROTEIN	19%
FAT	5% / 1 gm
CARBOHYDRATE	76%
SODIUM	556 mg

PASTA PRIMAVERA

MARINATED BAKED TOFU

PASTA PRIMAVERA

4 cups cooked pasta (approximately 2 cups uncooked)

Hint: Use an interestingly shaped pasta such as curly vegetable pasta or shells, spirals or bows. Spinach Fettuccini can also be used in this.

2 cups or more lightly steamed vegetables such as broccoli, cauliflower, carrots, onions, red or green peppers, and fresh or canned mushrooms

Note: The 2 cups measure is after cooking—this would probably be about 4 cups raw vegetables.

¾ cup cashew nuts

2 cups water

2 Tbs. food yeast flakes

1 Tbs. McKay's Chicken Seasoning

1 Tbs. lemon juice

½ tsp. garlic powder

½ Tbs. onion powder

1 ½ tsp. salt

3/4 tsp. paprika

3 Tbs. cornstarch

2 cups water

2 cups Marinated Baked Tofu (p. 47), opt.

1. Boil and drain pasta according to package directions.

2. Steam vegetables in a small amount of water and set aside.

3. While vegetables and pasta are cooking, blend cashew nuts with 2 cups water and all the seasonings and cornstarch for about 2 minutes, or until smooth.

4. Pour into a saucepan and add remaining 2 cups water. Bring to a boil, stirring constantly.

5. Fold together the cooked pasta, steamed vegetables, and sauce.

6. May be served immediately or placed in a casserole dish and sprinkled with seasoned bread crumbs and baked in a 350° degree oven until topping browns.

Prep. time: 30 min.
Cooking time: 20 min.
Baking time (opt.): 30 min.

Makes 6 - 8 servings of Pasta

Nutrient Information
Per Serving

CALORIES	196
PROTEIN	12%
FAT	29% / 6.4 gm
CARBOHYDRATE	59%
SODIUM	678 mg

MARINATED, BAKED TOFU

1 - 16 oz. brick tofu

2 Tbs. Bragg's Liquid Aminos or 1 Tbs. soy sauce

1 Tbs. McKay's Chicken Seasoning

1. Dice the tofu and place in a bowl with the seasonings. Toss to coat evenly.

2. Place seasoned tofu on an oiled or Pam-sprayed cookie sheet and bake at 400° for 10-15 minutes, or until lightly browned.

Serving Tip: Use in Stir-Fried vegetables, Pot Pie, or in any recipe to take the place of chicken.

Make extra and freeze. The texture will become even more chewy, and meaty when frozen

Makes 8 servings Baked Tofu

Nutrient Information
Per Serving

CALORIES	93
PROTEIN	40%
FAT	49% / 5.5 gm
CARBOHYDRATE	11%
SODIUM	313 mg

Entrees—Pasta and Tofu Dishes

VEGGIE QUICHE

VEGGIE PIZZA

VEGGIE QUICHE

1 cup water

1 lb. tofu

2½ Tbs. cornstarch

1 Tbs. lemon juice

1 Tbs. Vege-Sal or 1½ tsp. salt

½ tsp. oregano

1¼ tsp. basil

¼ tsp. savory

¼ tsp. garlic powder

¼ tsp. dill weed

1½ tsp. McKay's Chicken Seasoning

1 cup grated raw carrot*

1½ cups grated raw zucchini*

1 cup diced onion

*This is also very good using a 10 oz. pkg. of frozen, chopped spinach in place of the carrot and zucchini

1. Place all but last 3 ingredients in a blender and blend until smooth.

2. Place blended mixture in a large mixing bowl and stir in the grated vegetables and onion. Place in a 9 inch un-baked pie shell and bake at 350° for 50 minutes.

Hint: Another delicious variation is to use 1 cup frozen chopped spinach (thawed and drained), and ⅓ cup diced red pepper in place of the carrot and zucchini.

Serving Tip: Top may be garnished while hot with Tahini Cheese and parsley flakes or chives.

Prep. time: 40 min. (Including making pie crust) Cooking time: 50 min.

VEGGIE PIZZA

1 - 12 inch Pizza Crust (See Fruit Pizza for crust, p. 105)

¾ cup Tahini Cheese (p. 105)

1 cup Pasta Sauce (p . 45)

1 cup finely diced onions, green, red, and yellow bell peppers, etc.

¼ cup sliced olives

¼ cup mushrooms

1 cup shredded white Sliceable Cashew Cheese, opt. (p. 104)

VEGGIE PIZZA, cont'd.

1. Pre-bake the pizza crust until just beginning to brown.

Pizza crusts keep well in the freezer; also try English Muffins, Mediterranean flat bread or plain bread.

2. Spread pizza crust with ¾ cup of Tahini Cheese, covering entire surface.

3. Spoon the Pasta Sauce over the cheese and swirl it gently into the cheese.

4. Scatter surface with veggies, mushrooms, olives.

5. Bake just before serving for about 10 minutes at 350°

Hint: This can be assembled several hours or a day ahead and baked just before mealtime for a quick entree. You can even freeze the assembled pizza for future use if desired.

Prep. time: 20 min. (Add more time if you have to make crust and cheeses) Baking time: 10 min.

Option: A nice finishing touch is a sprinkle of shredded Cashew Cheese over the top!

Makes 8 servings

Nutrient Information
Per Serving

CALORIES	228
PROTEIN	21%
FAT	39% / 10.5 gm
CARBOHYDRATE	40%
SODIUM	815 mg

Makes 6 - 8 servings

Nutrient Information
Per Serving (1/8th of pizza)

CALORIES	123
PROTEIN	12%
FAT	56% / 8 gm
CARBOHYDRATE	32%
SODIUM	653 mg

LUNCHTIME FARE

Here you will find recipes to help you make those traditional lunch-time favorites such as burgers and sandwiches. Most of these are a great meal-in-one to take on a picnic or serve with soup or fruit.

Photo key:
1. **Cream of Broccoli Soup**
2. **Garden Sandwich**
3. **Tofu-Cottage Cheese**

Lunchtime Fare—Burgers

All of these burgers have been served with success at Five Loaves. The Vegeburger patty evolved from the "Meat Loaf Patties" recipe in *Something Better,** now made with bulgur wheat for simplicity instead of cooked wheat berries. You can make it with either. Sunburgers are made from Oat Burger patties and the Tahini Cheese makes it into a "cheeseburger." Rich in aroma and flavor, our Hickory Burger—a later addition to our menu—was an instant success.

VEGEBURGER

"Those who eat flesh are but eating grains and vegetables at second hand; for the animal receives from these things the nutrition that produces growth. The life that was in the grains and vegetables passes into the eater. We receive it by eating the flesh of the animal. How much better to get it direct, by eating the food that God provided for our use!" *Ministry of Healing,* p. 313

**Companion cookbook published by Neva Brackett, et. al.*

VEGEBURGERS

1½ cups water

2½ Tbs. Bragg's Liquid
Aminos or soy sauce

½ Tbs. Kitchen Bouquet

1 Tbs. Bernard Jensen's
Vegetable Gravy
Seasoning

1 tsp. sage

1 tsp. paprika

1 tsp. garlic powder

1 tsp. salt

1 large onion, peeled and
quartered

1½ cups Bulgur wheat

1 cup sunflower seeds
blended in 2 cups water

1 cup quick oatmeal

½ cup whole wheat or
white flour

⅓ cup gluten flour

1. Place 1½ cups water,
seasonings, and quar-
tered onion in blender
and blend briefly, just
long enough to chop the
onion. Pour into a sauce
pan and add bulgur
wheat. Bring to a boil,
cover and let stand for 10
minutes.

2. Meanwhile blend
sunflower seeds and
water, and place in a mixing bowl with the

remaining ingredients.
Mix all together.

3. Make into patties with
a scant ½ cup in each.

*Hint: An easy and quick
method is to place by the
scoopful with an ice cream
scoop onto a pre-heated,
non-stick griddle. Flatten
into round, ½ inch thick
patties. An alternate
method is to bake them in
the oven on a cookie sheet.*

4. Fry for about 7 minutes
on both sides, or bake for
about 20 minutes at 350°
(until browned on the
bottom). Turn and bake
10 more minutes to
brown both sides. Cool
on a rack before storing
in plastic bags or
container.

*Hint: Unless you have a
non-stick griddle or cookie-
sheet that is in good condi-
tion, you will have to coat
the surface with Pam.
Keep the temperature of
your griddle just above
medium, and don't let the
patties brown too fast. You
want them to cook in the
middle as well as on the
surface before turning
them.*

*Hint: This is a large recipe
and will make about 16
patties, 4 inches in diameter.
Extra patties can be frozen
for future use, or cut recipe
in half if desired.*

5. To make Vegeburgers,
split open a burger bun
and place Tofu Mayon-
naise (p. 89) on both sides.
Mustard Spread (p. 91)
may be used on one side if
desired. On bottom bun
place the burger patty,
Ketchup Spread (p. 91),
pickle slices, sliced tomatoes, lettuce or sprouts,
and top bun. It's even
better if you toast the
inside of the buns first
on a griddle or under
the broiler.

*Prep. time: 20 min.
Cooking time: 30 min.*

Makes 16 burger patties

Nutrient Information
Per Serving (1 patty)

CALORIES	159
PROTEIN	14%
FAT	28% / 5.2 gm
CARBOHYDRATE	58%
SODIUM	330 mg

Lunchtime Fare—Burgers

OATBURGER

TOFU GRILLER

OATBURGER

3 cups water

¼ cup soy sauce

1 Tbs. Dr. Bronner's
   Seasoning or,
   1Pkg Geo. Washington
   Broth, or
   1 Tbs. McKay's Beef
   Seasoning

3 Tbs. yeast flakes

1 tsp. sage

1 tsp. basil

1 tsp. Wright's Hickory
   Seasoning

1 tsp. garlic powder

½ Tbs. onion powder

¼ cup dry onion flakes or
   1 onion diced

½ tsp. salt

3 cups quick oats

½ cup ground walnuts or
   pecans

1. Place all ingredients in a saucepan except oats and nuts; simmer together for 3 minutes. Remove from heat and stir in quick oats and nuts. Allow sufficient cooling to handle in next step.

2. Shape into burger-sized patties—use a ½ cup ice cream scoop if available—and place on a non-stick or Pam-sprayed cookie sheet.

3. Bake at 375° until browned on both sides, or brown on a non-stick griddle.

Prep. time: 30 min.
Cooking time: 30 min.

TOFU GRILLER

3 cups water

⅓ cup McKay's Chicken
   Seasoning

½ tsp. garlic powder

2 - 16 oz.bricks tofu,
   sliced in ½ inch slabs

1. Place water and seasonings in a kettle or microwave container. Gently immerse the tofu slices into the seasoned water and bring to a boil. Simmer for 10 minutes.

2. Preheat teflon griddle and brown tofu on both sides.

Hint: May be browned on a cookie sheet in the oven instead of griddle if desired.

3. Serve in burger buns with avocado, salsa, tomato, lettuce, and mayonnaise.

Prep. time: 15 min.
Cooking time: 20 min.

Makes 12 burgers

Nutrient Information
Per Serving (1 patty)

CALORIES	48
PROTEIN	18%
FAT	48% / 2.7 gm
CARBOHYDRATE	34%
SODIUM	600 mg

Makes 8 servings

Nutrient Information
Per Serving (1 patty)

CALORIES	157
PROTEIN	40%
FAT	49% / 9.4 gm
CARBOHYDRATE	11%
SODIUM	222 mg

SUNBURGER

6 burger buns

6 Oatburger patties (p. 52)

1 red or mild sweet onion

2 large tomatoes

12 pitted olives

2 cups Tahini Cheese
(p. 105)

Tofu Mayonnaise (p. 89)

Vege-Sal

1. Place buns open-face
on a cookie sheet. Toast
briefly under broiler un-
til slightly browned.

2. Spread each with Tofu
Mayonnaise, then a
sprinkle of Vege-Sal, and
then the following:

   1 thin onion slice

   1 tomato slice

   1 Oatburger

   2 Tbs. Tahini Cheese

3. Secure each Sunburger
with a large wooden
toothpick down the
center. Bake at 400° for
about 20 minutes or until
the Tahini Cheese is

beginning to show a few
spots of browning.

4. Remove from oven and
garnish by placing a
whole olive over
toothpick; serve hot.

Prep. time: 20 min.
Cooking time: 15 min.

Makes 6 servings

Nutrient Information
Per Serving (1 burger)

CALORIES	149
PROTEIN	18%
FAT	27% / 4.8 gm
CARBOHYDRATE	55%
SODIUM	961 mg

BREADED EGGPLANT BURGER

BREADED, SLICED EGGPLANT*

1 eggplant, sliced about ¼ inch thick

8 oz. tofu

3 cups water

½ cup whole wheat or brown rice flour

½ tsp. salt

1. Blend all ingredients except eggplant in blender until smooth.

2. Place in a medium-sized bowl. This will be used for dipping eggplant.

Hint: An alternate sauce for dipping eggplant is Tofu Mayonnaise which you thin down slightly with water.

3. Make Seasoned Breading Meal (see below) and place some of it in a shallow bowl for dipping, adding more as needed.

This patty is for the burger but also works nicely as a side dish.

4. Dip raw eggplant slices first in the tofu mixture and then in the breading meal.

5. Place breaded eggplant slices on a cookie sheet and bake about 20 minutes at 375°, or until golden brown.

Hint: Slices may need to be turned to have them evenly browned. These may be made ahead and frozen to keep on hand for sandwiches or as a tasty accompaniment to any meal.

Note: This recipe is enough to dip and bread approximately 16 slices of eggplant.

Prep. time: 40 min.
Cooking time: 20 min.

SEASONED BREADING MEAL

2 cups fresh bread crumbs (can be made in blender or food processor)

½ tsp. paprika

1 tsp. onion powder

½ tsp. marjoram

½ tsp. thyme

1 tsp. salt

EGGPLANT BURGERS

6 burger buns

12 or more baked, breaded eggplant slices

Sliced White Cashew Cheese (p. 104)

Salsa

Tofu Mayonnaise (p. 89)

Sliced tomatoes

Green leaf lettuce

Alfalfa sprouts if desired

1. Toast or warm burger buns and spread with Tofu Mayonnaise.

2. Place desired number of eggplant slices on the bottom bun, and top with salsa; then a slice or two of cashew cheese, tomatoes, sprouts, and lettuce.

Prep. time: 20 min.

Makes 6 - servings

Nutrient Information
Per Serving (1 slice)
CALORIES 189
PROTEIN 16%
FAT 15% / 3.3 gm
CARBOHYDRATE 69%
SODIUM 226 mg

Makes 6 burgers

Nutrient Information
Per Serving (1 burger)
CALORIES 397
PROTEIN 15%
FAT 20% / 9.1 gm
CARBOHYDRATE 65%
SODIUM 784 mg

HICKORY BURGER

LENTIL COLD CUTS

HICKORY BURGER

1 - 16 oz. brick tofu

1 cup water

2 Tbs. Bragg's Liquid Aminos

2 cups whole wheat or spelt bread crumbs

¾ cup ground walnuts

¾ cup quick oats

½ cup dried onion flakes

1 tsp. garlic powder

1½ tsp. onion powder

½ Tbs. Vege-Sal

1½ tsp. salt

2 tsp. Wright's Hickory Seasoning

1 ½ tsp. Kitchen Bouquet

1 Tbs. molasses

½ cup sesame seeds

1½ cups cooked quinoa, (p. 37) millet or rice.

1. Blend tofu, water, and Liquid Aminos until smooth.

2. Mix together all the remaining dry ingredients in a large mixing bowl. Add the blended tofu and mix well.

3. Scoop onto a non-stick or Pam-sprayed cookie sheet with an ice cream scoop. Flatten with a spatula to ½ inch thick.

4. Bake at 350° until cooked and browned. Serve with Barbecue Sauce (p. 102).

Prep. time: 20 min.
Baking time: 30 min.

LENTIL COLD CUTS

1½ cups dry lentils

4½ cups water

1¼ cups chopped onions

2 cloves garlic

1 Tbs. onion powder

2 tsp. salt

1 tsp. Italian Seasoning

¼ cup tomato paste

2 Tbs. food yeast flakes

2 Tbs. Bragg's Liquid Aminos

1 Tbs. molasses

1 tsp. Hickory Seasoning

1. Place onions in a kettle with 1 cup of the water. Add the onion powder, garlic and salt. Bring to a boil and simmer for 5 minutes.

2. Meanwhuile, blend smooth lentils and remaining water. Add to simmering onions along with remaining seasonings. Bring to a boil and reduce heat; Simmer for 5 minutes, stirring constantly.

Hint: It's best to use a teflon-coated kettle to prevent sticking or burning this thick mixture.

3. Place in a sprayed 46 oz. juice can or loaf pan and chill. Remove by cutting end of can off and pushing contents out other end.

You may also use other sprayed molds. Slice and serve on whole grain bread with sprouts, Tofu Mayonnaise, tomato slices, onion, etc.

Makes 12-16 burger patties

Nutrient Information
Per Serving (1 patty)

CALORIES	166
PROTEIN	20%
FAT	44% / 8.6 gm
CARBOHYDRATE	36%
SODIUM	402 mg

Makes 30 cold cuts

Nutrient Information
Per Serving (1 slice)

CALORIES	41
PROTEIN	23%
FAT	3% / 0 gm
CARBOHYDRATE	68%
SODIUM	102 mg

Lunchtime Fare—Sandwiches

Now and then an uninformed customer will come in and ask for a turkey sandwich. When we explain that we serve only vegetarian food and show them our sandwich menu, they will sometimes order our Garden Sandwich, loaded with good things like avocados, tomatoes, sprouts, and sunflower seeds. But more often they give us that "oh-no-not-this-kinda-place" look, and quickly leave saying, "I've gotta have meat!" How sad, we think—if only they could know the poor trade-off they are making to satisfy a certain acquired taste!

GARDEN SANDWICH

"The moral evils of a flesh diet are not less marked than are the physical ills. Flesh food is injurious to health, and whatever affects the body has a corresponding effect on the mind and the soul. Think of the cruelty to animals that meat eating involves, and its effect on those who inflict and those who behold it. How it destroys the tenderness with which we should regard these creatures of God!" *The Ministry of Healing,* p. 315

FALAFIL POCKET SANDWICH

6 whole wheat pita halves

Tofu Mayonnaise (p. 89)

Hummus Tahini (p. 92)

24 Falafil balls (p. 58)

Sliced olives

Diced tomatoes

Shredded lettuce or
  alfalfa sprouts

1. Open pita half and
spread bottom with Tofu
Mayonnaise.

2. Place a large piece of
green leafy lettuce next
and top with 4 Falafil
balls, 2 or 3 spoonfuls of
Hummus Tahini, sliced
olives, diced tomatoes,
and stuff the remaining
space with shredded
lettuce or alfalfa sprouts.

*What are falafils? They
are a favorite Middle
Eastern filling for pocket
bread. Usually they are
made of pureed garbanzos
and hot spices, fried in hot
oil. We think you'll be
delighted with this light
and savory oven-baked version of an old favorite.*

Makes 1 Pocket Sandwich

Nutrient Information
Per Serving

CALORIES	319
PROTEIN	14%
FAT	19% / 6.7 gm
CARBOHYDRATE	67%
SODIUM	904 mg

Lunchtime Fare—Sandwiches

FALAFILS

GARDEN SANDWICH

FALAFIL

1 can (2 cups) garbanzo beans

¼ cup Do-pep or gluten flour (may use ½ cup corn flour)

½ cup soft bread crumbs

1 tsp. cumin

2 tsp. McKay's Chicken-like Seasoning (or ½ tsp. salt)

1 tsp. garlic powder

2 tsp. onion powder

½ tsp. salt

¼ cup dried onion flakes

⅓ cup ground walnuts

1. Mash garbanzos with a fork or in a food processor.

2. Combine remaining ingredients in a separate bowl.

Hint: It is important to mix the gluten flour with bread crumbs and season-ings before adding to the wet ingredients, otherwise the gluten flour will clump together if moistened in its concentrated form.

3. Add mashed garbanzos and liquid and mix with hands. Form into balls about the size of walnuts. If mix is too dry, add a bit of water.

4. Place on a non-stick cookie sheet and bake for 30 - 40 minutes at 350° until lightly browned. May be frozen.

Prep. time: 30 min.
Baking time: 40 min.

GARDEN SANDWICH

Whole wheat bread

½ large avocado

Sliced tomato

Green leaf lettuce

Thinly sliced cucumber

Toasted sunflower seeds

Vegetable seasoned salt

Alfalfa sprouts

Tofu Mayonnaise (p. 89)

1. Spread Tofu Mayonnaise on two slices of bread.

2. On one side place slices of avocado and sprinkle with Vege-Sal and toasted sunflower seeds. Add the remaining ingredients in the following order:

sliced tomato
sliced cucumber
lots of sprouts
leaf lettuce
top piece of bread

3. Slice in half and secure with large sandwich picks, or wrap for a sack lunch.

Makes 24 balls

Nutrient Information
Per Serving (3 balls)

CALORIES	162
PROTEIN	15%
FAT	21% / 4.1 gm
CARBOHYDRATE	64%
SODIUM	497 mg

Nutrient Information
Per Serving (½ sandwich)

CALORIES	363
PROTEIN	14%
FAT	55% / 23.9 gm
CARBOHYDRATE	31%
SODIUM	318 mg

Lunchtime Fare—Sandwiches

CHEESY SANDWICHES

SANDWICH SPREADS

CHEESY SANDWICHES

Whole wheat bread of your choice

Sliced Yellow Cashew Cheese (p. 104)

Spinach leaves, watercress, or lettuce

Low-calorie Mayonnaise (p. 81)

Sliced olives or pickles

Prepare each sandwich with 2 slices of bread, spread with Mayonnaise, a slice of cheese and lettuce or greens. May also add sliced olives or pickles. Use plastic wrap and pack in box lunch.

GRILLED TAHINI CHEESE ON RYE

Spread slices of rye bread with Tahini Cheese. Place on a cookie sheet and bake at 425° for 5 - 8 minutes—until cheese melts and bubbles a bit on the edges. Serve with soup.

SPINACH CHEESE ON FRENCH BREAD

1 loaf French bread
1 recipe Spinach Filling (p. 11)

Spread Spinach Filling on slices of French bread and place on cookie sheet. Bake at 425° for about 8 minutes. Serve hot with Spaghetti.

VEGGIE SANDWICH SPREAD

2 cups canned or cooked garbanzos

1 medium sized carrot, sliced and cooked

½ cup diced celery

⅓ cup peanut butter

1½ tsp. onion powder

½ tsp. dill weed

⅛ tsp. celery seed

¼ cup diced pickles

1 Tbs. pickle juice

½ tsp. salt

¼ cup finely diced red or green pepper

½ cup Tofu Mayonnaise (p. 89)

1. Mash the garbanzos and carrot with a fork, potato masher or in a food processor.

2. Stir in the remaining ingredients and mix well, adding more or less Tofu Mayonnaise to the desired consistency.

3. Spread 2 slices of bread lightly with Tofu Mayonnaise, and a generous layer of Sandwich Spread. Add lettuce or sprouts.

Prep. time: 20 min.

BEAN SPREAD OR DIP

1 cup cooked beans, mashed (pinto, black, red, pink, or kidney)

½ cup Tofu Mayonnaise (p. 89)

¼ cup Ketchup Spread (p. 91)

1 tsp. onion powder

½ tsp. garlic powder

Mix together and spread on your favorite bread.

Prep. time: 10 min.

ALMOND-OLIVE SPREAD

1 cup raw almonds

1 cup pitted olives

1 ½ cups water

1 tsp. salt

1 tsp. onion powder

½ tsp. garlic powder

Blend smooth in blender, adding more or less water as needed to make a spreadable consistency. Good on Rye Krisp or bread.

Veggie Spread makes 3 cups	
Nutrient Information	
Per Serving (¼ cup)	
CALORIES	110
PROTEIN	17%
FAT	36% / 4.6 gm
CARBOHYDRATE	47%
SODIUM	344 mg

Bean Spread makes 1½ cups	
Nutrient Information	
Per Serving (2 Tbs.)	
CALORIES	69
PROTEIN	22%
FAT	14% / 1.5 gm
CARBOHYDRATE	64%
SODIUM	370 mg

Lunchtime Fare—Soups

A steamimg bowl of vegetable soup—what could be more appealing on a cold winter evening? It surely "hits the spot" but you may want to keep in mind some of the suggestions we printed concerning soup in *Something Better.**

Our stomachs generally prepare for an expected meal making enzymes, acid and many constituents at just the right concentration. If very much water, for example, is taken during the meal, or even following it too closely, the digestive process will proceed more slowly and less completely because of dilution. In fact, with any significant liquid taken during the meal, including fruit or vegetable juice, there is a simlar increase in the time required for digestion.

How does this relate to soup? If one consumes from one to three cups of water with a relatively small amount of nutrients, as in a bowl of soup, slower or poor digestion can result. Generally, soup is not "chewed" and thus the initiation of the digestive process during mastication is also bypassed. This may relate to juicing any foods (even whole!) since the "juice" is usually not chewed as is best for good digestion. And finally, excess liquid requires considerable salt for flavor.

What to do? Soup need not be eliminated perhaps, but the use of crackers, zwieback, rye crisp or bread sticks with the soup give it more body. Soup also can be made thick and chunky, by using a little less water. So, enjoy your less-soupy soup!

**First cookbook published by Neva Brackett and Evelyn Earl*

CHILI

4 cups dry small red beans

1 - 6 oz. can tomato paste

2 Tbs. cumin

1 Tbs. garlic powder

1 Tbs. paprika

1 Tbs. basil

½ Tbs. oregano

2 Tbs. cilantro

1 Tbs. onion powder

1- 48 oz. can V-8 juice

1 cup dry vegetarian
   burger or bulgur wheat

¼ cup fruit juice sweetener
   or honey

1 diced green pepper

1 diced onion

½ Tbs. Vege-Sal or 1 tsp. salt

¼ cup Bragg's Liquid
   Aminos

1. Soak beans overnight or bring to a boil and soak 1 hour in the hot water; drain.

2. Cover beans with fresh water 1 inch above the beans. Add seasonings and cook for about 4 hours or until tender.

Hint: You can make this with pinto beans in about half the cooking time—about 2 hours, but your "chili" will be more pale in color.

3. In a separate kettle, simmer onion, green pepper, burger or bulgur wheat, and V-8 juice together for about 10 or 15 minutes until tender.

4. Add to cooked beans and serve hot.

Hint: This is very good made in a crock pot by placing all ingredients in the pot with boiling water. Let cook for 8 to 12 hours depending on the kind of beans. Cook and add the vegetables at the last if you want to preserve their color and texture.

Prep. time: 15 min.
Cooking time: approx. 4 hr.

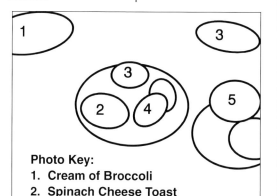

Photo Key:
1. **Cream of Broccoli**
2. **Spinach Cheese Toast**
3. **Chili**
4. **Grilled Tahini Cheese on Rye**
5. **Sunburgers**

Makes 4 quarts

Nutrient Information
Per Serving (1 cup)

CALORIES	312
PROTEIN	17%
FAT	1% /.5 gm
CARBOHYDRATE	82%
SODIUM	64 mg

CORN CHOWDER

SPLIT PEA SOUP

CORN CHOWDER

2 medium potatoes

1 medium onion

1 green pepper

½ tsp. salt

1 Tbs. McKay's Chicken
Seasoning

½ tsp. garlic powder

1½ tsp. savory

¼ tsp. basil

½ tsp. celery salt

¾ cup cashews

2 cups water

1 cup well-cooked rice or
¼ cup potato flour

¼ cup fresh parsley, or
1 Tbs. dried parsley

4 cups corn

2 cups water

1. Dice onion, pepper and potatoes and place in a large kettle with 4 cups water. Bring to a boil and simmer until tender while adding the seasonings.

2. Blend cashews, water, and rice or potato flour until smooth. Add the fresh parsley and blend for a few seconds at the end to chop.

3. Add blended cashew mixture to cooked potatoes and onions.

4. Place 2 cups of the corn in the blender with 2 cups of water. Blend and add to soup in kettle along with the remaining 2 cups of whole corn. Add more salt according to your taste. Heat, but don't boil as texture may become curdled.
Serve hot.

Prep. time: 30 min.
Cooking time: 15 min.

SPLIT PEA SOUP

3 cups dry split peas

8 cups water

1 large onion

1 small carrot

1½ tsp. salt

2 Tbs. yeast flakes

1 Tbs. McKay's Chicken
Seasoning

½ tsp. savory

1 tsp. celery salt

½ tsp. Wright's Hickory
Seasoning

½ tsp. garlic powder

½ tsp. paprika

½ tsp. dill weed

Cook 1¼ hours and then blend smooth.
Serve hot.

Prep. time: 15 min.
Cooking time: 1 hr. 15 min.

Makes 12 cups

Nutrient Information
Per Serving (1 cup)

CALORIES	132
PROTEIN	11%
FAT	26% / 4.2 gm
CARBOHYDRATE	63%
SODIUM	342 mg

Makes 8 cups

Nutrient Information
Per Serving (1 cup)

CALORIES	263
PROTEIN	27%
FAT	3% / .9 gm
CARBOHYDRATE	70%
SODIUM	473 mg

Lunchtime Fare—Soups

CREAM OF BROCCOLI

CREAM OF ZUCCHINI

CREAM OF BROCCOLI

6 cups raw broccoli pieces

1 medium onion, diced

½ cup red pepper, diced

3 cups water

1½ tsp. salt

½ tsp. garlic powder

1 tsp. savory

1 Tbs. McKay's Chicken Seasoning

¾ cups cashews

2 cups water

1 cup well-cooked rice, or 1 large cooked potato, or ¼ cup potato flour

1. Place onion in kettle with 3 cups water and seasonings. Simmer 10 minutes and then add the broccoli and diced red pepper. Simmer 5 minutes till tender, but still bright green.

2. Meanwhile blend cashews, potato or rice in 2 cups water until smooth.

3. Add blended cashew mixture to cooked broccoli and serve hot.

Prep. time: 20 min.
Cooking time: 15 min.

CREAM SAUCE*

1 large or 2 medium potatoes, well cooked

2 cups water

½ cup cashews

½ tsp. garlic powder

½ to 1 tsp. salt to taste

*Used in Cream of Zucchini Soup

CREAM OF ZUCCHINI

1 large potato, cubed

2 stalks celery, sliced

1 onion, diced

1 medium sized zucchini, quartered and sliced

¼ cup diced red pepper

2 Tbs. McKay's Chicken Seasoning

½ tsp. summer savory

4 cups water

1. Place above ingredients in a large saucepan and bring to a boil. Reduce heat and simmer until vegetables are tender.

2. Meanwhile, blend together the Cream Sauce (see middle column) until smooth; then stir into the cooked vegetables. Heat until steaming hot, but not boiling. If allowed to boil, the cream sauce will become curdled in appearance.

Prep. time: 20 min.
Cooking time: 15 min.

Makes 9 cups

Nutrient Information
Per Serving (1 cup)
CALORIES	94
PROTEIN	15%
FAT	34% / 3.9 gm
CARBOHYDRATE	51%
SODIUM	491 mg

Makes 12 cups

Nutrient Information
Per Serving (1 cup)
CALORIES	54
PROTEIN	10%
FAT	42% / 2.7 gm
CARBOHYDRATE	48%
SODIUM	302 mg

Lunchtime Fare—Soups

CHUNKY VEGETABLE

CHUNKY VEGETABLE

2 small potatoes, diced

1 medium carrot, sliced

1 onion, diced

2 cups cabbage, diced

2 stalks celery with leaves

1 can wax or green beans

Water to cover vegetables

2 tsp. dill weed

¼ cup soy sauce

1 Tbs. McKay's Chicken Seasoning

¼ tsp. marjoram

½ tsp. basil

½ tsp. savory

¼ tsp. thyme

1 large can V-8 juice

Cook all ingredients except the V-8 juice until just done, but don't overcook (cabbage should not be limp). Add V-8 last. Serve hot.

Prep. time: 30 min.
Cooking time: 25 min.

Makes 9 cups

Nutrient Information
Per Serving (1 cup)

CALORIES	72
PROTEIN	12%
FAT	3% / .3 gm
CARBOHYDRATE	85%
SODIUM	865 mg

MEXICAN

MEXICAN

1 - 4 oz. can sliced olives

1 - 4 oz. can mushroom pieces

1 - 10 oz. pkg. frozen corn

¼ tsp. garlic powder

½ tsp. cumin

1 large can V-8 juice

2 cans red kidney beans

1 large onion, chopped

1 - 20 oz. can diced tomatoes

1 bell pepper, diced

1 cup dry macaroni noodles

1. Place onion and bell pepper in a large kettle with the large can of diced tomatoes. Bring to a boil and simmer 5 minutes.

2. Add remaining ingredients and bring to a boil. Simmer for about 15 minutes until all ingredients are cooked including the macaroni.

Makes 12 cups

Nutrient Information
Per Serving (½ cup)

CALORIES	137
PROTEIN	16%
FAT	4% / .3 gm
CARBOHYDRATE	80%
SODIUM	491 mg

ARMENIAN LENTIL

ARMENIAN LENTIL

1½ cups lentils

10 cups water

½ cup brown rice

1 cup diced onions

1 cup frozen chopped spinach

2 cups diced or stewed tomatoes

2 Tbs. lemon juice

2 Tbs. Braggs Liquid Aminos

1 Tbs. onion powder

1 Tbs. salt

1 Tbs. McKay's Chicken Seasoning

1 tsp. garlic powder

1 tsp. dill weed

2 tsp. cumin

½ tsp. basil

1. Place all ingredients in kettle except brown rice and cook for 30 minutes.

2. Add rice and cook for 45 minutes longer. Serve hot.

Prep. time: 20 min.
Cooking time: 1 hr. 15 min.

Makes 12 cups

Nutrient Information
Per Serving (1 cup)

CALORIES	62
PROTEIN	13%
FAT	4% / .3 gm
CARBOHYDRATE	83%
SODIUM	418 mg

BLACK BEAN SOUP

1 large potato, peeled and diced

2 stalks celery, diced

1 med. onion, diced

1 cups diced tomatoes, canned or fresh

¼ tsp. garlic powder

½ tsp. cumin

½ tsp. dill weed

1 Tbs. yeast flakes

1 tsp. salt (or less to taste)

2 cups water

1 cup cooked brown rice

⅓ cup cashew nuts

1 cup water

2 cups cooked black beans

1. Place potatoes, celery, tomatoes, seasonings, and water in a large kettle and cook together for about 20 minutes, or until vegetables are tender.

2. Meanwhile blend together the cooked rice and cashews with 2 cups water until smooth; add to the cooked vegetables along with the black beans and heat together until serving temperature. It is best not to let it come to a full boil.

Prep. time: 20 min.
Cooking time: 20 min.

Makes 8 cups

Nutrient Information
Per Serving (1 cup)
CALORIES 150
PROTEIN 16%
FAT 19% / 3.2 gm
CARBOHYDRATE 65%
SODIUM 384 mg

Lunchtime Fare—Soups

CREAM OF TOMATO

SPANISH TOMATO RICE

CREAM OF TOMATO

½ cup cashews

1½ cups well cooked rice

2 cups water

3 cups tomatoes, canned diced pieces or fresh

¼ cup honey or conc. fruit juice sweetener

½ tsp. salt

1½ Tbs. McKay's Chicken Seasoning

¼ tsp. savory

¼ tsp. dill weed

2 cups water

1. Blend cashews and rice with 2 cups water until smooth.

2. Pour blended cashews in large kettle; then blend tomatoes until smooth.

3. Add blended tomatoes to cashew mixture in kettle along with remaining ingredients.

4. Heat almost to a boil, but don't let it boil or the texture may become curdled. Serve hot.

Prep. time: 15 min.
Cooking time: 10 min.

SPANISH TOMATO-RICE

½ cup uncooked rice

8 cups water

3 cups carrots, diced

1 green pepper, diced

1 onion, diced

4 cups celery, diced

4 cups canned tomatoes in puree

1 Tbs. salt

½ tsp. garlic powder

2 tsp. cumin

1 tsp. Italian seasoning

2 Tbs. molasses

1 cup Tahini Cheese (p. 105)

1. Dice pepper, carrots, onion, and celery and place in a large kettle with water and uncooked rice and all remaining ingredients except Tahini Cheese. Bring to a boil and simmer 40 min. Add 1 - 2 cups water if needed.

2. Remove from heat and stir in Tahini Cheese. Serve.

Makes 8 cups

Nutrient Information
Per Serving (1 cup)

CALORIES	149
PROTEIN	8%
FAT	26% / 4.5 gm
CARBOHYDRATE	66%
SODIUM	278 mg

Makes 16 cups

Nutrient Information
Per Serving (1 cup)

CALORIES	75
PROTEIN	10%
FAT	20% / 1.7 gm
CARBOHYDRATE	70%
SODIUM	532 mg

GARDEN AND ORCHARD

$\mathbf{F}$amilies and institutions should learn to do more in the cultivation and improvement of land. If people only knew the value of the products of the ground, which the earth brings forth in their season, more diligent efforts would be made to cultivate the soil. All should be acquainted with the special value of fruits and vegetables fresh from the orchard and garden." *Counsels on Diet and Foods,* p. 312

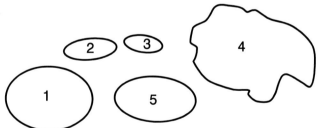

Photo key:
1. **Broccoli and Cauliflower Au Gratin**
2. **Green beans with Vegetable Seasoning Sauce**
3. **Zucchini Creole**
4. **Garden veggies**
5. **Mashed Potatoes, Zucchini Creole with tomato wedges**

Garden and Orchard—Vegetables

We present here only a few of the many vegetable recipes we have used, simply to give you some basic principles. Once you learn how to prepare appealing vegetable dishes without dairy or oil, you can pick out any recipe of your choice and adapt it according to these principles.

Spicy Yam Bake and Zucchini Creole

Spicy Yam Bake

Zucchini Creole

SPICY YAM BAKE

3 lb. yams or sweet potatoes

⅓ cup pure maple syrup or ¼ cup honey

½ tsp. cardamom

½ tsp. coriander

1¼ cup raisins

1 cup Cashew Milk*

2 tsp. vanilla

12 - 15 pecan halves

¾ tsp. salt to taste

1. Steam yams until thoroughly cooked and soft.

2. Mash peeled yams and add all ingredients, stirring in the amount of milk needed to make a nice moist texture.

Hint: A quick way to make this is to place the cooked yams and the remaining ingredients (except the raisins) in a food processor, and whiz until well mashed.

*Or your choice of "milks" from soy, etc.—p. 19-21

3. Turn into a 1½ quart casserole dish and garnish top with pecans if desired.

4. Bake at 350° for 25 - 30 minutes.

Prep. time: 15 min.
Cooking and baking time: 1 hr.

Makes 5 cups

Nutrient Information
Per Serving (½ cup)

CALORIES	188
PROTEIN	6%
FAT	2% / gm
CARBOHYDRATE	92%
SODIUM	227 mg

ZUCCHINI CREOLE

8 cups sliced green and yellow zucchini

1 cup diced onion

1 green pepper, diced

1 clove garlic

¾ cup water

1 tsp. salt

1 tsp. Italian seasoning

½ tsp. dill weed

1 Tbs. McKay's Chicken Seasoning

1- 2 Tbs. cornstarch dissolved in ¼ cup water

3 cups diced fresh tomatoes

1. Place all ingredients except tomatoes and cornstarch in a saucepan and cook about 8 minutes, until zucchini gets tender.

2. Add tomatoes and stir in dissolved cornstarch. Stir as the sauce comes to a boil and thickens. Serve hot.

Prep. time: 20 min.
Cooking time: 10 min.

Makes 8 cups

Nutrient Information
Per Serving (1 cup)

CALORIES	52
PROTEIN	16%
FAT	7% /.5 gm
CARBOHYDRATE	77%
SODIUM	453 mg

MASHED POTATOES

CREAMED PEAS

MASHED POTATOES

12 cups pared and quartered Russet potatoes

Approx. 8 cups water

1½ tsp. salt

2 or more cups Cashew Milk (p. 20) or a non-sweet soy milk

1. Place potatoes and water in a large kettle and bring to a boil. Reduce heat and simmer until very well cooked, about ½ hour.

Hint: Russet potatoes, those rough, brown-skinned potatoes we usually use for baking, are best for mashing because they cook soft and mash softer and smoother than the red or white potatoes which are firm and tend to mash starchy and lumpy.

2. Remove from heat and drain off all of the water.

3. Mash with a potato masher or use an electric mixer. Add cashew or soy milk and salt to taste, adding as much milk as needed for the consistency you like.

Hint: It is important to mash the potatoes immediately after removing them from the stove. If you let them sit before mashing them, they will become starchy and your mashed potatoes will have a gummy texture.

Prep. time: 15 min.
Cooking time: 30 min.

CREAMED PEAS

2 cups Cashew Milk (p. 20) or Soy Milk (p. 19)

3 Tbs. flour or cornstarch

1 tsp. salt

2 - 10½ oz. pkgs. frozen peas, thawed

1. Put flour and salt in saucepan. Add cold milk slowly, stirring until smooth.

Hint: Place milk in blender with salt and flour and blend briefly to mix in for lump-free cream sauce.

2. Cook until thickened, stirring frequently. Add thawed peas and heat just to desired serving temperature. Serve immediately.

Hint: A good way to thaw the peas is to cover them with hot water and let them sit for 5 min., then drain.

Variation: Add 4 cups diced, cooked potatoes and 1 pkg. peas for creamed potatoes and peas.

Makes 10 cups

Nutrient Information
Per Serving (1 cup)
CALORIES	162
PROTEIN	10%
FAT	10% / 1.8 gm
CARBOHYDRATE	80%
SODIUM	331 mg

Makes 8 servings

Nutrient Information
Per Serving
CALORIES	73
PROTEIN	21%
FAT	17% / 1.5 gm
CARBOHYDRATE	62%
SODIUM	320 mg

Garden and Orchard—Vegetables

BROCCOLI AU GRATIN

VEGETABLE SEASONING SAUCE

BROCCOLI-CAULIFLOWER TIPS AU GRATIN

1 bunch broccoli (usually 3 heads are bound together in a bunch)

1 head cauliflower

1 cups Cheesy Sauce (p. 105)

1. Pick out broccoli that is fresh—dark green and firm. Cut off bottom half of stems and discard. Cut each bunch lengthwise into 3 or 4 long stems with heads.

2. Cut and trim cauliflower into individual flowerettes.

3. Steam broccoli and cauliflower together in a vegetable steamer or in a kettle with a small amount of water.

Remove lid to let steam escape after they are half cooked to prevent broccoli from discoloring.

Return lid and steam until tender, but being careful not to overcook. Test if done with a sharp knife or fork.

4. Arrange broccoli on an oven-proof platter or baking dish with heads outward and stems inward. Arrange cauliflower in the center. Drizzle with Cheesy Sauce. May serve immediately or prepare ahead and place in oven or microwave to heat before serving. Garnish with red bell pepper half-circles if available.

Prep. time: 15-20 min.
Cooking time: 10 min.

VEGETABLE SEASONING SAUCE

2 cups water

3 Tbs. lemon juice

2 Tbs. honey

2 Tbs. dry onion flakes, opt.

1 tsp. salt

1 Tbs. McKay's Chicken Seasoning

2 tsp. basil

¼ tsp. garlic

3 Tbs. cornstarch

1. Mix all together in a saucepan except dissolved cornstarch.

2. Bring to a boil and slowly stir in the dissolved cornstarch.

3. Drizzle over hot steamed vegetables before serving (green beans, cabbage, cauliflower, carrots, peas, etc.).

This will enhance the flavor of your vegetables and give them eye appeal, taking the place of butter or margarine.

Makes 10

Nutrient Information
Per Serving

CALORIES	97
PROTEIN	31%
FAT	11% / 1.5 gm
CARBOHYDRATE	58%
SODIUM	124 mg

Makes 9 servings

Nutrient Information
Per Serving (¼ cup)

CALORIES	20
PROTEIN	3%
FAT	1% / 0 gm
CARBOHYDRATE	96%
SODIUM	395 mg

FRENCH FRIES

SCALLOPED POTATOES

FRENCH FRIES
(baked, not fried!)

1 large Russet baking
   potato

salt and paprika

1. Wash potato and slice
lengthwise into ½ inch
slices. Cut the slices into
french fry strips. (skin
may be left on)

2. Place in a Pyrex baking
dish or bowl and sprinkle
with salt and paprika to
taste. Toss until evenly
coated.

3. Place in microwave and
cook for approx. 5 minutes,
or until tender but not
shriveled or dry.

*Non-microwave option:
steam 10 minutes on the stove.*

4. Place pre-cooked potatoes
on a lightly oiled (sprayed)
cookie sheet and bake at
450° for approximately
15 minutes, or until
crispy brown and
puffy—watch carefully
so they don't burn.

5. Serve immediately with
Ketchup Spread (p. 91)
or Tofu Sour Cream dip
(p. 92).

*Tip: Potatoes may be baked
without pre-cooking in the
microwave, eliminating
step #3. But pre-cooking
both speeds the baking and
results in a nicer texture
and appearance.*

SCALLOPED POTATOES

5 cups peeled, sliced
   potatoes

1 large onion, thinly sliced

½ cup cashew nuts

3 cups water

1½ tsp. salt

1½ Tbs. flour or 1 Tbs.
   cornstarch

basil (opt.)

1. Cover potatoes with
water in a saucepan and
par boil (partially boil)
for 5 minutes. Drain off
water. May be used for
making the milk in step 3.

2. Meanwhile, steam
onions slightly in a small
pan with a small amount
of water.

3. Blend cashew nuts in
1 cup of the water until
smooth. Add remaining
2 cups of water and salt
and flour.

4. In a casserole dish that
has been sprayed with
Pam, place layers of potatoes and onions, sprinkle
layers with basil to taste
if desired. Pour cashew
milk mixture over all and
bake at 400° for 30 minutes,
or until lightly browned
on top and potatoes are
bubbling and tender.

Makes 2 servings

Nutrient Information
Per Serving

CALORIES	45
PROTEIN	10%
FAT	2% / .1 gm
CARBOHYDRATE	88%
SODIUM	270 mg

Makes 8 servings scallops

Nutrient Information
Per Serving

CALORIES	134
PROTEIN	10%
FAT	26% / 10 gm
CARBOHYDRATE	64%
SODIUM	407 mg

Garden and Orchard—Vegetables

POTATO-CARROT BAKE

POTATO-CARROT BAKE

4 medium sized potatoes

4 large carrots

1 large onion

Cashew Milk, approx. 3 cups (p. 20)

Salt to taste (approx. 1 tsp.)

1. Coarsely grate potatoes and carrots, and dice the onion.

> *Tip: The food processor is excellent for this—just place pieces of potato and carrots and onions in it, using the chopping blade, but not too many at a time. Pulse briefly until coarsely chopped.*

2. Mix together in a baking dish that has been coated with Pam and sprinkle with salt to taste. Pour Cashew Milk to about half way covering the potato mixture in the dish.

3. Bake at 400° for 45 minutes. Serve hot.

Makes 6 servings

Nutrient Information
Per Serving

CALORIES	155
PROTEIN	10%
FAT	30% / 5.5 gm
CARBOHYDRATE	60%
SODIUM	379 mg

MICROWAVE CHIPS

MICROWAVE CHIPS

1 raw potato

Tofu Seasoning to taste (p. 12) (about 1 tsp.)

1. Slice potato thinly and pat dry between paper towels to remove excess moisture.

2. Place a sheet of microwave wrap on a plate and a single layer of potato slices on the wrap.

3. Sprinkle potato slices with seasonings. Microwave on high 3 - 6 minutes.

Makes 1 servings

Nutrient Information
Per Serving (1 potato)

CALORIES	80
PROTEIN	9%
FAT	1% / 0 gm
CARBOHYDRATE	90%
SODIUM	119 mg

POTATO-CARROT SUPREME

POTATO-CARROT SUPREME

4 medium sized potatoes

4 large carrots

2 medium onions

1½ tsp. salt

Cashew Milk (p. 20)

1. Cut peeled carrots, onions, and potatoes into large pieces.

2. Boil with salt in just enough water to allow cooking. Cook until both potato and carrot are tender. Potatoes should be in larger pieces than carrot since the carrot takes a longer cooking period.

3. Add enough Cashew Milk to taste good and serve hot. This will surprise you in that it is so simple, yet well liked by all, especially the children.

Makes 8 servings

Nutrient Information
Per Serving

CALORIES	149
PROTEIN	10%
FAT	35% / 6 gm
CARBOHYDRATE	55%
SODIUM	419 mg

Garden and Orchard—Vegetables

POTATO POPPERS

VEGGIES with PASTA

POT PIE PERFECT

POTATO POPPERS

1 cup mashed potatoes

1 cup cooked brown rice

1 cup whole grain bread crumbs

¼ cup chopped onion

½ tsp. salt (or more if potatoes are not salted)

1 Tbs. tomato sauce

1. Simmer onion in a small amount of water.

2. Combine all ingredients and form into 1½ inch balls

3. Bake until delicately browned—about 15 minutes.

Variation for Pot Pie Perfect: Use Quick Cobbler Crust recipe (p. 121), omitting sweetener in the dough.

VEGGIES with PASTA

1 cubed green bell pepper

1 cubed red bell pepper

1 cup cubed yellow summer squash

1 cup cubed zucchini

2 cups cooked pasta

McKay's Chicken Seasoning

½ recipe Cheesy Sauce (p. 105)

1. Saute chopped peppers in water. Saute summer squash and zucchini with water in another pan.

2. Season with chicken-like seasoning (to taste). Layer pasta, squash, peppers.

3. Serve with hot Cheesy Sauce

POT PIE PERFECT

4 potatoes, cut in large pieces

3 carrots, sliced

1 large onion, diced

1 cup fresh or frozen peas

1 cup diced **Veggie Cutlets** (p. 31) or **Marinated, Baked Tofu** (p. 47)

5 cups **Mushroom Gravy** (p. 99)

Basic Pastry Dough (p. 124)

1. Cook vegetables (except peas) in a small amount of water until barely tender.

2. Place drained vegetables in a baking dish with 1 cup of frozen peas on top. Pour gravy over this.

3. Roll out Basic Pastry Dough ½ inch thick and place on top. This dough uses yeast, so will need to rise for 20-30 minutes until double.

4. Bake at 400° for 20 minutes then reduce heat to 250° for 15-20 minutes.

Variation: see left.

Makes 12 balls

Nutrient Information
Per Serving (2 balls)

CALORIES	95
PROTEIN	12%
FAT	6% / .7 gm
CARBOHYDRATE	82%
SODIUM	473 mg

Makes 3 cups

Nutrient Information
Per Serving (1 cup)

CALORIES	108
PROTEIN	16%
FAT	7% / 1 gm
CARBOHYDRATE	77%
SODIUM	10 mg

Makes 8 servings Pot Pie

Nutrient Information
Per Serving

CALORIES	310
PROTEIN	13%
FAT	20% / 7 gm
CARBOHYDRATE	67%
SODIUM	567 mg

Garden and Orchard—Vegetables

ALMOND STIR FRY

ALMOND STIR FRY

1 cup carrots, sliced in diagonal thin slices

1 cup cauliflower, thinly sliced

1 cup thin onion slices

1 cup green beans, cut into 1 inch pieces

1 cup water

2 Tbs. McKay's Chicken Seasoning or 1½ tsp. salt

½ tsp. garlic powder

1 Tbs. cornstarch

½ cup blanched, whole almonds

1. Cook vegetables in a small amount of water along with seasonings for about 5 minutes.

2. Mix cornstarch with a small amount of water and stir into simmering vegetables to thicken.

Serving Tip: Vegetables should be crisp. Serve over brown rice and top with almonds.

Makes 6 servings

Nutrient Information
Per Serving
CALORIES	155
PROTEIN	10%
FAT	30% / 5.5 gm
CARBOHYDRATE	60%
SODIUM	379 mg

DILLY CABBAGE

DILLY CABBAGE

1 head cabbage

1 tsp. dill weed

½ tsp. Vege-Sal

1. Chop cabbage—not too fine.

2. Cook in a wok or covered frying pan in a little water until done.

3. Season with dill weed and Vege-Sal and serve hot.

Makes 10 servings

Nutrient Information
Per Serving (1 cup)
CALORIES	26
PROTEIN	17%
FAT	6% / 0 gm
CARBOHYDRATE	77%
SODIUM	17 mg

GREEN BEAN DELIGHT

GREEN BEAN DELIGHT (WITH ONION)

3 cups green beans, cut in ½ inch pieces

1 onion, diced fine

½ tsp. oregano

½ clove garlic

1 cup water

1½ tsp. salt

½ tsp. savory

¼ tsp. dill weed

1. Wash and cut ends from beans. Hold several at a time on a cutting board and cut into small pieces (about ½ inch).

2. Place in a kettle with water and seasonings and cook until tender, about 15 - 20 minutes.

Makes 8 servings

Nutrient Information
Per Serving (½ cup)
CALORIES	27
PROTEIN	17%
FAT	3% / .1 gm
CARBOHYDRATE	80%
SODIUM	537 mg

Garden and Orchard—Salads

Nicely prepared vegetables and fruits in their season will be beneficial, if they are of the best quality, not showing the slightest sign of decay, but are sound and unaffected by any disease or decay." *Counsels on Diet and Foods*, p. 309

Clockwise from bottom: Winter Fruit Salad, Vege Pasta Salad and Potato Salad.

Garden and Orchard—Salads

WINTER FRUIT SALAD

SUMMER FRUIT SALAD

WINTER FRUIT SALAD

2 sweet apples

2 oranges

4 bananas

2 kiwi

1 cup red seedless grapes or frozen blueberries

½ cup frozen orange juice conc., thawed

½ cup frozen apple juice conc., thawed

1 cup water

3 Tbs. cornstarch or Instant Clear Jel

1. Mix together juices, water, and cornstarch dissolved in some of the water. Bring to a boil in a small saucepan. Pour into a shallow pan and chill for about an hour.

Or if you have Instant Clear Jel, place juices and water in blender and blend in the Clear Jel until the consistency of pudding. Does not need to be chilled.

2. Peel and dice small all the fruit. Add frozen blueberries or grapes.

3. Fold in the thickened juice and serve.

Prep. time: 25 min.

*This "topping" for Fruit Salad may be made with cornstarch:

Use 3 Tbs. cornstarch dissolved in a small amount of pineapple juice. Add the remaining juice and bring to a boil. Cool in refrigerator in a flat pan for an hour before stirring into the fruit.

SUMMER FRUIT SALAD

8 cups cut up fresh summer fruits, such as:
   cantaloupe
   honeydew
   grapes, red and green
   blueberries
   strawberries
   apricots
   cherries

1 ½ cups chilled apple or pineapple juice

2-3 Tbs. Instant Clear Jel* (see left column)

1. Place fruit juice in blender with 2 Tbs. Clear Jel. Turn on and blend briefly. Let sit for about 5 minutes to thicken.

2. Turn on blender and add more Clear Jel if needed to make a thick sauce the consistency of pudding. Stir into the fresh fruits and serve.

Makes 8 servings

Nutrient Information
Per Serving
CALORIES	181
PROTEIN	4%
FAT	3% / .7 gm
CARBOHYDRATE	93%
SODIUM	7 mg

Makes 8 servings

Nutrient Information
Per Serving
CALORIES	111
PROTEIN	5%
FAT	5% / .7 gm
CARBOHYDRATE	90%
SODIUM	10 mg

Garden and Orchard—Salads

FRUIT AMBROSIA

CREAMY WALDORF SALAD

FRUIT AMBROSIA

10 cups cut up fresh
   fruits in season or
   6 cups fruit cocktail
   canned in fruit juice

1 cup frozen blueberries
   or raspberries

2 bananas, sliced

1 apple, diced

¾ cups apple juice conc.

1¼ cup cold water

¼ tsp. coconut extract

⅓ cup Better Than Milk
   Lite* powder (or other
   soy milk product)

¼ cup Instant Clear Jel**

   *No added free fat in the
   "lite" version.

   **Or you could use ¼ cup
   cornstarch blended into the
   liquid as in Step #2, then
   bring to a boil as you stir
   (Instant Clear Jel needs no
   cooking to thicken).
   Remove to a flat metal pan
   and cool in refrigerator for
   about an hour before
   folding into the fruits.

1. Cut up the fruit into a
large mixing bowl.

2. Place apple juice in
blender with cold water,
coconut extract and milk
powder. Turn on and
while blending, add the
Clear Jel.

3. Fold blended sauce
into the fruits and serve.

   Prep. time: 30 min.

CREAMY WALDORF SALAD

6 Fuji apples (Red or
   Golden Delicious are
   next best)

1 cup diced celery

1 cup raisins or sliced,
   pitted dates

3/4 cup coarsely chopped
   roasted almonds,
   cashew nuts, or walnuts

1½ cups Whipped
   Topping (p. 156)

1 Tbs. fresh lemon juice

1. Quarter and core apples.
Slice each quarter into 5
or 6 thin slices and cut
slices once in half. Place
apples in a mixing bowl
and toss with fresh
lemon juice to keep from
browning.

2. Slice celery in thin,
diagonal slices and add
to apples.

3. Add remaining
ingredients. Serve as is
or chill for a nice effect
on warm days

Makes 12 servings

Nutrient Information
Per Serving (1 cup)
CALORIES   345
PROTEIN   9%
FAT   6% / gm
CARBOHYDRATE   85%
SODIUM   482 mg

Makes 10 servings

Nutrient Information
Per Serving
CALORIES   168
PROTEIN   7%
FAT   36% / 7 gm
CARBOHYDRATE   57%
SODIUM   25 mg

CRANBERRY-STRAWBERRY MOLD

2 cans (12 oz) frozen
  conc. apple juice
  (thawed)

2 cups fresh or frozen
  whole cranberries

1½ cups fresh or frozen
  whole strawberries

2 sticks agar (or ½ cup
  agar flakes)

1. Blend 1 can of conc.
apple juice with thawed
strawberries and cranber-
ries until smooth.

2. Pour into a saucepan
with the second can of
apple juice and 2 sticks
of agar broken into 1
inch pieces.

3. Bring to a full boil,
stirring occasionally, and
boil for 1 minute. Pour
into a nice looking glass
dish, and chill.

*Hint: This doesn't "unmold"
well. Just serve out of the
dish with a spoon—or use an
ice cream scoop for
individual servings on green
leafy lettuce on a separate
plate. This is a very delicious
cranberry sauce to serve at a
Thanksgiving-type meal.*

*Prep. time: 10 min.
Cooking time: 8 min.*

Set up time: 8 hr.

Makes 8 servings

Nutrient Information
Per Serving (½ cup)

CALORIES	174
PROTEIN	2%
FAT	2% / .5 gm
CARBOHYDRATE	96%
SODIUM	24 mg

Garden and Orchard—Salads

CUCUMBER SALAD

CUCUMBER SALAD

12 cups cucumbers

1¼ cups frozen orange juice conc., thawed

1 tsp. lemon juice

1½ tsp. dill weed

1½ tsp. salt

1 tsp. onion powder

½ tsp. garlic powder

1. Pare cucumbers and if desired, score with the tines of a fork; slice thinly.

2. Combine with all other ingredients.

3. Place in a covered container and leave overnight in the refrigerator to marinate. Leftover can be stored in the refrigerator and used for at least 2 weeks, so don't be afraid of making too much!

Prep. time: 15 min.
Marinating time:
at least 8 hr..

Makes 10 servings	
Nutrient Information	
Per Serving	
CALORIES	74
PROTEIN	8%
FAT	3% / .3 gm
CARBOHYDRATE	90%
SODIUM	323 mg

COUSCOUS SALAD

COUSCOUS or QUINOA SALAD

4 cups cooked couscous or quinoa (p. 33, 35)

½ green pepper, diced

½ red pepper, diced

2 green onions, sliced

2 large stalks celery, sliced

¾ cup sliced olives

½ cup toasted slivered almonds or cashews

1 cup Tahini Dressing (see next column)

Prep. time: 20 min.

Makes 12 servings

Makes 12 servings	
Nutrient Information	
Per Serving (¾ cup)	
CALORIES	349
PROTEIN	13%
FAT	21% / 8.3 gm
CARBOHYDRATE	66%
SODIUM	231 mg

TAHINI DRESSING

TAHINI DRESSING

1 cup water

2 Tbs. tahini

2 Tbs. lemon juice

2 Tbs. honey

½ tsp. garlic powder

1 tsp. salt

Mix dressing in a small bowl and stir into salad ingredients. You may need to add more salt if your Quinoa or Couscous was unsalted. This salad may be made ahead or served immediately.

Prep. time: 5 min.

Makes 1¼ cups	
Nutrient Information	
Per Serving (2 Tbs.)	
CALORIES	31
PROTEIN	6%
FAT	42% / 1.6 gm
CARBOHYDRATE	52%
SODIUM	217 mg

Garden and Orchard—Salads

POTATO SALAD

POTATO SALAD

10 medium sized potatoes, peeled and steamed

3 stalks of celery, diced

½ cup diced pickles (opt.)

½ green pepper, diced

½ red pepper, diced

1 cup green onions, sliced

1. For best results, choose red or new white potatoes. Steam for about 45 minutes, or until they are well cooked, and not at all crisp in the center. Let cool, and then dice.

2. Add remaining ingredients, and stir in one recipe of Potato Salad Dressing. The salt is in the dressing, so don't salt the potatoes while cooking.

Prep. time: 25 min.
Cooking time: 30 - 40 min.
Chilling time: 4 hr. or
overnight

Makes 10 servings

Nutrient Information
Per Serving (1 cup)
CALORIES   142
PROTEIN   9%
FAT   26% / 4.4 gm
CARBOHYDRATE   65%
SODIUM   655 mg

RUSSIAN POTATO SALAD

RUSSIAN POTATO SALAD

Add diced cooked beets, carrots and extra dill weed to basic Potato Salad.

POTATO SALAD DRESSING

POTATO SALAD DRESSING

2¼ cups water

1 cup cashews

¼ cup honey or conc. fruit sweetener

⅜ cup lemon juice

¾ tsp. dill weed

1½ Tbs. salt

2 tsp. onion powder

½ tsp. garlic powder

2 - 3 Tbs. potato flour

Blend all together until smooth—at least 2 minutes.

Make sure there are no cashew nut granules by feeling some of the mixture between your thumb and finger, and blend as long as necessary to make a smooth dressing.

The dressing will seem too
salty, but it is the right
amount when mixed with
the unsalted, cooked
potatoes.

Makes 3 3/4 cups

Nutrient Information
Per Serving (1 cup)
CALORIES   277
PROTEIN   5%
FAT   27% / 9.1 gm
CARBOHYDRATE   68%
SODIUM   464 mg

FOUR BEAN SALAD

CONFETTI PASTA SALAD

FOUR BEAN SALAD

1 cup each: garbanzos, kidney beans, green beans, wax beans

> *(or for variation try butter beans, pinto beans, and frozen green beans)*

½ cup raw sweet or red onion, diced (opt.)

½ cup red or green pepper, diced (opt.)

2 Tbs. lemon juice

1 Tbs. honey or 1 Tbs. each conc. orange juice and apple juice

1 tsp. onion powder

⅛ tsp. garlic powder

1 tsp. McKay's Chicken Seasoning

½ tsp. dill weed.

½ tsp. celery salt

Mix all together and chill several hours or overnight.

> *Prep. time: 10 min.*
>
> *Chilling time: Several hours or overnight*

CONFETTI PASTA SALAD

2 cups penne or other medium pasta, cooked and drained

3 small yellow crooked neck squash, sliced

2 small zucchini, cut in small Julienne strips

1 small red pepper, sliced thin

1 small yellow pepper, sliced thin

¼ cup thinly sliced red onion

¾ cup sliced or whole black pitted olives

1 cup Italian Dressing (p. 96)

Use extra salt to taste

Mix all together and chill at least 2 hours or overnight to allow the vegetables to absorb the flavors.

> *Prep. time: 20 min.*
> *Cooking time: 15 min.*
> *Chilling time: 2 hr. or overnight*

Makes 4 cups

Nutrient Information
Per Serving (½ cup)

CALORIES	84
PROTEIN	17%
FAT	6% / .5 gm
CARBOHYDRATE	77%
SODIUM	333 mg

Makes 10 cups

Nutrient Information
Per Serving (1 cup)

CALORIES	131
PROTEIN	12%
FAT	6% / 1 gm
CARBOHYDRATE	82%
SODIUM	190 mg

VEGETABLE MEDLEY SALAD

2 cups vegetable pasta spirals, cooked and drained

6 cups broccoli flowerettes with some broccoli stems, cut up

4 cups zucchini, cut in shoe string strips

½ red pepper, cut in thin 1-inch strips

1 can sliced water chestnuts, cut smaller

1 ½ cups Potato Salad Dressing (p. 81)

1 tsp. dill weed

Salt to taste (about 1 tsp.)

1. Place broccoli and zucchini in a steamer or sauce pan with a small amount of water. Steam just until crisp-cooked, but still bright green.

2. Combine steamed vegetables with cooked pasta and remaining ingredients.

3. Chill in refrigerator for at least 2 hours or overnight before serving.

Hint: The pasta spirals tend to absorb moisture, so before serving the salad you may need to stir in a half cup or more of water if it has lost its creamy, moist appearance. Don't be afraid to do this—it works wonders for a pasta salad that looks too dry!

Prep. time: 20 min.
Cooking time: 15 min.
Chilling time: 2 hours or more

Makes 10 servings

Nutrient Information
Per Serving (1 cup)

CALORIES	144
PROTEIN	12%
FAT	17% / 3 gm
CARBOHYDRATE	71%
SODIUM	370 mg

Garden and Orchard—Salads

TOFU COTTAGE CHEESE

COLESLAW

TOFU COTTAGE CHEESE

1 brick tofu (16 oz.)

1 cup Tofu Sour Cream (p. 92)

1 Tbs. dried chives (or 2 Tbs. fresh)

2 tsp. onion powder

½ tsp. salt

¼ tsp. garlic powder

1. Mash tofu with a fork and stir in remaining ingredients.

2. Chill or serve on a green leaf lettuce or in stuffed tomatoes.

Prep. time: 10 min.
Makes 3 cups

COLESLAW

1 medium head cabbage (about 8 -9 cups shredded)

½ cup tofu

⅓ cup pineapple juice

1 cup crushed pineapple, drained

1 Tbs. lemon juice

1 Tbs. honey

1 tsp. Vege Sal (or increase salt to 3 tsp.)

2 tsp. salt

1 Tbs. parsley flakes

1. Blend tofu with pineapple juice and seasonings. Stir into finely shredded cabbage and crushed pineapple.

2. May be served now, but better if allowed to sit for several hours in the refrigerator before serving.

Makes 3 cups

Nutrient Information
Per Serving (½ cup)

CALORIES	157
PROTEIN	39%
FAT	48% / 9.2 gm
CARBOHYDRATE	13%
SODIUM	406 mg

Makes 8 cups

Nutrient Information
Per Serving (¾ cup)

CALORIES	97
PROTEIN	21%
FAT	27% / 2.9 gm
CARBOHYDRATE	52%
SODIUM	421 mg

TOPPINGS

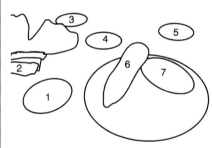

Photo key:
1. Guacamole
2. Cashew Cheese
3. Millet Butter
4. Tofu Sour Cream
5. Italian Dressing
6. Millet Butter on Corn
7. Tofu Sour Cream / Potato

We often hear the comment, "If only I had a good recipe for mayonnaise—that's my biggest problem." Mayonnaise is so basic to the American diet. We use it in salads, dressings, on sandwiches and in dips. The following low-fat recipes are great replacements we find virtually everyone is happy to use!

Toppings—Spreads

ere is a subtle problem that most of us struggle with
when it comes to changing our diet, because what we
put on our food to give it more moisture and flavor,
can double, triple, or quadruple the calories! The fact is that
spreads and dressings (butter, margarine, mayonnaise, etc.) are
normally high in fat, but they don't have to be. You can still
transform plain baked potatoes into a mouth-watering entree,
topped with all the guilt-free Millet Butter and Tofu Sour
Cream needed to make it delicious and appetizing. When you
grasp the basic concepts in this section, you make a giant step,
for many of our entrees, salads, and soups are simply variations
on these themes.

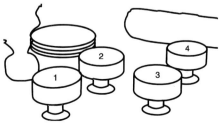

Photo key:
1. **Millet Butter**
2. **Guacamole**
3. **Fresh Raspberry Jam**
4. **Tofu Sour Cream**

Toppings—Spreads

FRESH RASPBERRY JAM

2 cups fresh or frozen, thawed raspberries or blackberries (4 cups frozen berries will melt down to 2 cups when thawed.)

1 - 16 oz. can (2 cups) conc. apple juice

⅓ cup Instant Clear Jel or ⅓ cup cornstarch dissolved in ⅓ cup water

CLEAR JEL METHOD

l. Place apple juice, water, and Clear Jel in blender, along with the juice drained off the thawed berries. Turn on low and blend for about ½ minute. Turn off and let stand 5 minutes.

Hint: It should be the consistency of pudding after standing. If it appears thinner than that, add another tablespoon of Clear Jel, blend and let stand a minute longer. For a thicker jam use more Clear Jel, or for a sauce to put over ice cream or tapioca pudding, use less.

2. Add the thawed berries. Turn the blender on low speed for a few seconds— only enough to stir in the berries. Too much blending will cause it to be seedy.

Hint: Be sure the berries are not still frozen or the jam will look opaque and frothy.

CORNSTARCH METHOD

l. Place apple juice conc. and juice from thawed berries in a saucepan and bring to a boil.

2. Remove pan from heat and immediately stir dissolved cornstarch into hot apple juice, adding in a slow stream while stirring constantly. Return to heat and bring to a boil while stirring, then remove from heat. It should be the consistency of pudding.

3. Put in refrigerator for about an hour and then stir in the thawed raspberries. For best results, don't add the raspberries while boiling hot or the berries will cook and lose their fresh taste and color.

Prep. time: 10 min.

Note: Fresh Raspberry Jam does not freeze well!

Cooking time: 10 min.
Chilling time: 4 hr.

COOKED BERRY JAM

COOKED BERRY JAM

1 - 16 oz. pkg. (about 4 cups) frozen blackberries, Marionberries, or strawberries, thawed

1 stick agar (or 3 Tbs. agar flakes, or 3 tsp. agar powder)

1 - 12 oz. can frozen apple juice concentrate

1. With juice in blender, break agar stick in pieces into blender Cover and blend briefly.

2. Add thawed berries and blend very briefly to simply chop berries without breaking the seeds out of their pockets.

3. Pour into a saucepan and bring to a full rolling boil; boil for 1 minute.

4. Put in containers, chill.

It will be a runny consistency when hot, but will set up when chilled. May be frozen or poured into hot sterilized jars for canning.

Cooking time: 10 min.
Chilling time: 4 hr.

Makes 4 cups

Nutrient Information
Per Serving (1 Tbs.)

CALORIES	9
PROTEIN	13%
FAT	3% / 0 gm.
CARBOHYDRATE	84%
SODIUM	1 mg

Toppings—Spreads

ORANGE-APPLE MARMALADE

2 cups very thinly sliced oranges with peeling

3 cups dried apples

1 cup conc. orange juice

2½ cups conc. apple juice

3 cups water

1. Slice oranges, not in whole slices, but more as orange marmalade— very, very thin.

2. Place half the dried apples in the blender with 2½ cups conc. apple juice. Blend only until chopped fine, but not blended smooth. Repeat with remaining apples and water.

3. Place all ingredients in large kettle or crockpot. Cook slowly for about 1 hour (4-6 hr. in a crock-pot) or until oranges are tender. May be frozen or canned.

Prep. time: 25 min.
Cooking time: 1 hr.

Makes 7 cups

Nutrient Information
Per Serving (1 Tbs.)

CALORIES	44
PROTEIN	3%
FAT	2% / .9 gm.
CARBOHYDRATE	95%
SODIUM	8 mg

YOLANDA'S BETTER BUTTER

YOLANDA'S
BETTER BUTTER

½ cup raw blanched almonds

1 Tbs. Emes Kosher Jel

1½ cups hot water

1½ cups hot cooked millet

1 small cooked carrot

1½ tsp. salt

2 drops butter flavoring, opt.

⅛ tsp. guar gum or xanthan gum, opt.

1. Blend almonds with jel and water until very smooth

2. Add rest of ingredients and continue blending until smooth.

3. Pour into storage containers

4. Chill. Use as butter!

Note: The carrot gives color to Better Butter. Depending on the carrots, use more or less as needed.

Makes 3½ cups

Nutrient Information
Per Serving (1 Tbs.)

CALORIES	26
PROTEIN	15%
FAT	27% / 1 gm.
CARBOHYDRATE	58%
SODIUM	1 mg

Toppings—Spreads

TOFU MAYONNAISE

CASHEW MAYONNAISE

TOFU MAYONNAISE

1 - 16 oz. brick tofu or 12 oz. Mori-Nu tofu and ⅓ cups cashews

½ cup water or more

¼ cup lemon juice

⅓ cup conc. fruit juice sweetener or honey or ⅓ cup pineapple-orange juice concentrate.

2¼ tsp. salt

1 Tbs. onion powder**

2 - 4 Tbs. potato flour*

1. Blend together until smooth all ingredients except potato flour, adding just enough water so the tofu will blend. Soft tofu will usually blend without adding water.

2. While blender is running, add 2 Tbs. potato flour* and continue blending about 30 seconds for mix to thicken.

Hint: Since some potato flour is more starchy than others, the amount needed will vary. Add more to achieve a thicker mayonnaise.

3. Blend about 30 seconds more after the last of the potato flour has been added to make it look smooth and satiny. Insufficient blending will result in a mealy appearance from the potato flour. Too much potato flour will make it gummy and starchy, so learn to find the right balance.

Prep. time: 10 min.

*Make sure you are using potato flour, not potato starch. There is an important difference! (see appendix)

Hint: Keep in mind that if either mayonnaise has become quite warm in blending, it will be slightly thicker when chilled.

Tofu or Cashew Mayonnaise will keep nearly two weeks when refrigerated. They can be frozen (to keep indefinitely), but when thawed need re-blending, adding potato flour as needed to give a nice consistency.

**For the discriminating chef, there are two kinds of onion powder. One is a very fine powder (with better flavor results), the other is granulated.

CASHEW MAYONNAISE*

¾ cup cashew nuts

For longer "shelf life" cover nuts with water, bring to boil, drain and rinse (the microwave is handy for this)

2 cups water

¼ cup lemon juice

⅓ cup conc. fruit juice sweetener or honey

2¼ tsp. salt

1 Tbs. onion powder**

4 - 5 Tbs. potato flour

1. Blend together all ingredients except potato flour about 1 minute.

2. Continue blending an additional minute while adding potato flour (see both step #3 and the hint after step #2 in Tofu Mayonnaise).

Prep. time: 10 min.

*Note: This is a variation of Tofu Mayonnaise. All the flavorings are the same, except using cashew nuts and water instead of tofu.

Makes 3½ cups

Nutrient Information
Per Serving (1 Tbs.)

CALORIES	21
PROTEIN	23%
FAT	31% / .8 gm.
CARBOHYDRATE	44%
SODIUM	87 mg

Makes 3½ cups

Nutrient Information
Per Serving (1 Tbs.)

CALORIES	21
PROTEIN	7%
FAT	35% / .9 gm.
CARBOHYDRATE	58%
SODIUM	86 mg

Toppings—Spreads

MILLET BUTTER

MANDARIN COCONUT BUTTER

MILLET BUTTER

½ cup millet cooked in 2½ cups water for 30 minutes.*

3 cups boiling water

2½ Tbs. unflavored Emes Kosher Jel

¼ cup cashews

2 Tbs. Shilling Butter Flavored Salt

1 Tbs. lemon juice

1 Tbs. honey or conc. fruit juice sweetener

1. Dissolve Emes in boiling water.

2. Place hot millet in blender with half the boiling water mixture and the remaining ingredients. With lid on blender, cover with a towel, hold in place and start blender. Blend smooth—about 2 minutes (as blender starts, hot liquid may forcefully open lid and splash operator with its scalding contents).

*or ½ cup corn meal in 2 cups of water for only 5 minutes.

Before turning blender off, add remaining water mixture.

Hint: This works best if blended when the millet is still hot off the stove. It does not work as well to use cold, re-heated millet.

3. Pour into containers and chill before serving.

Hint: It is quite runny when hot, but will thicken to a spreadable consistency when chilled. This is an excellent substitute for butter on toast, baked potatoes, or vegetables (very good on corn on the cob) because it melts, moistens, and tastes very good. Not very suitable on popcorn and not to be used as a substitute for butter or margarine in baking pastries or cookies.

Note: Keeps for 2 weeks. Freezing will change the texture, but can be fixed by boiling again in the microwave or on the stove, stir or blend, then chill to set up.

Prep. time: 10 min.
Cooking time: 30 min.

Variation: For a more creamy "butter," either double the cashews to ½ cup or add 2 Tbs. powdered lecithin. This adds fat, of course, but the result is a little more like margarine as a transition for those who need it.

MANDARIN-COCONUT BUTTER

Follow Millet Butter directions with these substitutions:

1. Reduce boiling water to 1 cup.

2. Add 2 whole mandarin oranges* (including peel) to the blender.

3. Add 1 cup coconut milk and 1 tsp. coconut flavoring.

4. Increase honey to ½ cup.

You may substitute a whole medium orange with about ¼ of the peel

---

Makes 6 cups

Nutrient Information
Per Serving (1 Tbs.)

CALORIES	7
PROTEIN	14%
FAT	30% / .2 gm.
CARBOHYDRATE	56%
SODIUM	mg

Makes 5 cups

Nutrient Information
Per Serving (2 Tbs.)

CALORIES	14
PROTEIN	10%
FAT	51% / .8 gm.
CARBOHYDRATE	39%
SODIUM	89 mg

KETCHUP

MUSTARD SPREAD

KETCHUP

2 cups tomato sauce

1 - 6 oz can tomato paste

¼ cup fruit sweetener

2½ Tbs. lemon juice

2 Tbs. Bragg's Liquid Aminos or Soy Sauce

1½ tsp. salt

½ tsp. celery salt

½ tsp. basil

1. Blend all ingredients together until smooth.

2. Place in a sauce pan. Bring to a boil and simmer for 20 minutes, stirring occasionally. Chill or serve hot. May be frozen.

Hint: You will likely be tempted to skip the cooking step and use the ketchup uncooked. It is still good this way, but cooking improves the flavor and sterilizes it so that it keeps at least twice as long in the refrigerator.

Prep. time: 10 min.
Cooking time: 20 min.

Makes 3½ cups

Nutrient Information
Per Serving (1 Tbs.)

CALORIES	6
PROTEIN	9%
FAT	4% / 0 gm.
CARBOHYDRATE	87%
SODIUM	65 mg

MUSTARD SPREAD

1 cup water

¼ cup cashews

1 Tbs. cornstarch

1 scant tsp. turmeric

½ tsp. paprika

¾ tsp. salt

2 tsp. onion powder

½ tsp. garlic powder

1 Tbs. lemon juice

1. Blend all ingredients together for about 2 minutes.

2. Place in a saucepan and bring to a boil, stirring constantly. Chill before serving.

Prep. time: 15 min.
Cooking time: 10 min.

Makes 1 cup

Nutrient Information
Per Serving (1 Tbs.)

CALORIES	16
PROTEIN	9%
FAT	53% / 1 gm.
CARBOHYDRATE	38%
SODIUM	98 mg

Toppings—Spreads

TOFU SOUR CREAM

TOFU SOUR CREAM

1 - 16 oz. brick tofu

¼ cup water

3 Tbs. lemon juice

½ tsp. garlic powder

2 tsp. onion powder

1½ tsp. salt

1 Tbs. dried or fresh chives

1. Blend all ingredients except chives until smooth.

Hint: Depending on the firmness of your tofu, you may need to add more water to get the desired consistency of sour cream. If you are using pasteurized boxed tofu or soft tofu, you should use no water.

2. Add the dried chives and blend very briefly just to stir them in, but not to puree them.

Serving tip: Use as a topping on baked potatoes, Cuban Black Beans, broccoli, greens, or as dip for raw vegetables or chips.

Prep. time: 10 min.

Makes 2½ cups

Nutrient Information
Per Serving (1 Tbs.)
CALORIES	12
PROTEIN	38%
FAT	46% / .7 gm.
CARBOHYDRATE	16%
SODIUM	81 mg

GUACAMOLE

GUACAMOLE

2 medium avocados, peeled and quartered

1 cup tofu

½ cup water

½ tsp. garlic powder

½ tsp. salt (or more to taste)

1 tsp. onion powder

1 Tbs. lemon juice

1. Place tofu in blender along with one of the avocados and remaining ingredients; blend until creamy.

2. Meanwhile, mash remaining avocado with a fork and then stir in the blended avocado mixture. Serve as a dip or on Soft Tacos or Burritos.

Prep. time: 10 min.

Makes 2½ cups

Nutrient Information
Per Serving (1 Tbs.)
CALORIES	99
PROTEIN	18%
FAT	68% / 8 gm.
CARBOHYDRATE	14%
SODIUM	115 mg

HUMMUS TAHINI

HUMMUS TAHINI

2 cups cooked garbanzos (1-15 oz. can)

½ cup tahini (Joyva brand is best)

⅓ cup lemon juice

1 clove garlic or ½ tsp. garlic powder

salt to taste (½ to 1 tsp.)

¼ tsp. dill weed

½ to 1 cup water (or juice from canned garbanzos)

Blend all together in blender, adding water in the amount needed to the thickness desired. Blend until smooth, about 1 minute.

Prep. time: 5 min.

Makes 3 /12 cups

Nutrient Information
Per Serving (1 Tbs.)
CALORIES	25
PROTEIN	16%
FAT	44% / 7.1 gm.
CARBOHYDRATE	40%
SODIUM	41 mg

STRAWBERRY-PINEAPPLE SPREAD

4 cups unsweetened
   whole strawberries
   (fresh or frozen)*

apple juice or water as
   needed

approx. 1-2 cups diced,
   dried pineapple

1. Blend berries into a
puree.

   *Frozen berries should be
   thawed. They will have
   enough liquid for blending, whereas fresh berries
   will usually require a little
   water or apple juice.*

2. While the berries are
blending, add dried pine-
apple a little at a time
until the blend becomes
thick enough to spread
on bread without being
too runny.

3. Serve as a spread for
bread or rolls, or use as a
delicious light dessert
topping.

   *Measure frozen strawberries
   before thawing.*

*Serving Tip: An easy and
light dessert idea is to coat
sliced bananas and pineapple
chunks with orange juice
concentrate, spoon into a
dessert dish and top with
Strawberry-Pineapple
Spread and Whipped
Topping (p. 156) or
shredded coconut.*

*Variation: Any fresh or
frozen, thawed berries can
be made into a delicious
spread by blending with
fruit juice and adding
dried pineapple or dried
apples until a spreadable
consistency.*

*Another very tasty spread
can be made by blending 1
cup of applesauce with ½
cup of dried pitted prunes.
For extra flavor add ½ tsp.
each of coriander and
maple flavoring.*

Makes 4-5 cups

Nutrient Information
Per Serving (4 Tbs.)

CALORIES	68
PROTEIN	2%
FAT	2% / .3 gm.
CARBOHYDRATE	96%
SODIUM	323 mg

FAT CONTENT IN WHOLE PLANT FOODS

100 gram Portions (3.5 oz.)	% Cal as Fat	Total Cal	Total Fat (gm)	Portion of fat as		
				Poly Unsat	Mono Unsat	Sat
Pecans	91.3	667	67.6	16.8	42.2	5.4
Brazil Nuts	90.9	656	66.2	24.1	23.0	16.2
Avocado	88.1	177	17.33	2.04	11.2	2.6
Walnuts	86.7	642	61.9	39.1	14.2	5.6
Almonds	80.0	587	52.2	11.0	33.9	5.0
Peanuts	78.4	570	49.7	15.7	24.6	6.9
Sunflower Seeds	78.3	570	49.6	32.7	9.5	5.2
Olives	76.3	81	6.9	0.6	5.1	0.9
Cashews	72.7	574	46.4	7.8	27.3	9.2
Soybeans	40.9	141	6.4	3.55	0.72	0.7

There are essentially only four categories of whole plant foods which are considered "high" in fat: Nuts, olives, avocados and seeds! These and a sampling of the the more common nuts are included here along with soybeans, a fairly high-fat food outside of the main four. They are arranged in descending order of percentage of total calories as fat. The reason that avocados and olives are so low in total calories is that they are mostly water (on the order of 85% for olives!) whereas for the nuts only several per-cent of their weight is water. So, if you ate enough olives to get as many calories as, say, pecans, you'd have 57 grams of fat, not far behind the nuts.

Mono-unsaturated fat is probably the safest form to have in the diet and you can see that these "natural" products are rich in mono, relatively low in saturated and fairly low in poly-unsaturated. Good food! Fat in the diet is necessary for good health—it just needs to be from the right place in not too large a quantity.

It's better also to get the fat from plants than from animals for many reasons among which is they are high in saturated fat which makes the user at risk for heart disease. It's also wise to get the fat from the plant, eaten in the plant rather than being taken out of the plant and eaten as visible or "free" fat. Anytime fat is taken out of it's natural protective "envelope," it is subject to oxidization, creating "free radicals" which damage the DNA our body's cells. Too much poly-unsaturated fat tends to put us at risk for malignant neoplasms (cancer) so the answer is to eat the whole plant, unrefined! Many people feel it is best to use extra-virgin, cold-pressed olive oil if any free fat is to be used. "Extra" refers to a "level" above "virgin" in the extraction process which in a practical sense means very little of the olive is discarded—a good plan!

DRESSINGS

Most salad dressings you buy are not only high in fat, but also vinegar, an acid that irritates the digestive tract. Our dressings combine lemon, apple, and orange juices for a delightful sweet-sour flavor that is better than vinegar!

Millet Butter melting deliciously on steaming corn, baked potato smothered with Tofu Sour Cream and a tossed salad with Italian Dressing.

"'Something better' is the watchword of education, the law of all true living. Whatever Christ asks us to renounce, He offers in its stead *SOMETHING BETTER*."

E. G White, *Education*, p. 296

Toppings—Dressings

FRENCH

ITALIAN

GREEK OLIVE

FRENCH DRESSING

1½ cup water

¼ cup orange juice conc.

½ cup apple juice conc.

½ cup lemon juice

3 Tbs. tomato puree

1 tsp. dill weed

1 tsp. onion

1 tsp. garlic

1 tsp. paprika

1½ Tbs. salt

1½ Tbs. cornstarch
   dissolved in ¼ cup water

1. Place all except dissolved cornstarch in saucepan and bring to a boil.

2. Stir in cornstarch water, and cook 1 minute. Chill before serving

Tip: Both the French and Italian Dressing recipes will keep for several months in the refrigerator without spoiling, so don't be afraid to make a whole recipe.

Prep. time: 10 min.
Cooking time: 5 min.

ITALIAN DRESSING

2½ cups water

½ cup conc. orange juice

¾ cup conc. apple juice

½ cup lemon juice

¼ tsp. savory

¼ tsp. rosemary

½ tsp. basil

½ tsp. dill weed

4 tsp. onion powder

2 tsp. garlic powder

2 tsp. Vege-Sal

2 tsp. salt

2 Tbs. cornstarch
   dissolved in ½ cup water

1. Bring all but corn-starch water to a boil.

2. Gradually stir in the cornstarch water and boil 1 minute. Chill. Keeps 2 or 3 months in the refrigerator.

Prep. time: 10 min.
Cooking time: 5 min.

GREEK OLIVE DRESSING

¼ cup lemon juice

½ cup orange juice conc.

1 cup water

½ cup pitted black or green, ripe olives

3 Tbs. conc. fruit sweetener or honey

1 tsp. lime juice (opt.)

½ fresh onion, or ½ Tbs. onion powder

½ Tbs. Vege-Sal

1 Tbs. salt

1 tsp. oregano

1 tsp. basil

½ tsp. garlic powder(scant)

⅛ tsp. rosemary

⅛ tsp. thyme

¼ tsp. dill weed

Blend all ingredients until smooth. Use directly on dark green salad.

Prep. time: 10 min.

Makes 3 cups

Nutrient Information
Per Serving (1 Tbs.)

CALORIES	13
PROTEIN	4%
FAT	2% / 0 gm.
CARBOHYDRATE	94%
SODIUM	206 mg

Makes 4 cups

Nutrient Information
Per Serving (1 Tbs.)

CALORIES	19
PROTEIN	3%
FAT	2% / 0 gm.
CARBOHYDRATE	95%
SODIUM	96 mg

Makes 2 cups

Nutrient Information
Per Serving (1 Tbs.)

CALORIES	24
PROTEIN	5%
FAT	7% / .2 gm.
CARBOHYDRATE	88%
SODIUM	281 mg

CREAMY CUCUMBER*

CREAMY CUCUMBER

10½ oz. pkg. tofu (1¼ cups)

½ cup water

3 Tbs. lemon juice

¼ cup conc. fruit sweetener or honey

½ cucumber, washed and un-peeled

½ tsp. garlic powder

½ tsp. basil

½ tsp. celery salt

2 tsp. salt

½ Tbs. onion powder

1 Tbs. potato flour

¼ cup sweet or green onions

1 avocado, opt.

1. Blend all ingredients together until smooth.

2. Chill and serve on tossed salad.

Variation: For a richer dressing, blend in 1 avocado Prep. time: 15 min.

*Courtesy of Rilla Klingbeil

Makes 2 ¾ c. (no avocado)

Nutrient Information
Per Serving (1 Tbs.)

CALORIES	13
PROTEIN	34%
FAT	41% / .63 gm.
CARBOHYDRATE	25%
SODIUM	123 mg

RANCH-STYLE

RANCH-STYLE

1 cup Tofu or Cashew Mayonnaise (p. 89)

¼ cup water

1 Tbs. lemon juice

¼ tsp. celery salt

1 tsp. onion powder

½ tsp. parsley

¼ tsp. poppy seed

¼ tsp. dill weed

¾ tsp. salt

⅛ tsp. garlic powder

⅛ tsp. sweet basil

Place Mayonnaise in a bowl and stir in the remaining ingredients.

Prep. time: 5 min.

Makes 1 1/3 cups

Nutrient Information
Per Serving (1 Tbs.)

CALORIES	9
PROTEIN	22%
FAT	26% / .3 gm.
CARBOHYDRATE	52%
SODIUM	81 mg

Toppings—Gravies and Sauces

In today's cooking, the essence of gravies and sauces is fat, salt and spices. We admit that no matter how carefully seasoned and skillfully prepared the new version of your old favorite, it won't taste the same. However, if you give it a chance, you will be surprised how quickly your taste will be won over to these light but satisfying foods.

"Persons who have indulged their appetite to eat freely of meat, highly seasoned gravies, and various kinds of rich cakes and preserves, cannot immediately relish a plain, wholesome, and nutritious diet. Their taste is so perverted that they have no appetite for a wholesome diet of fruits, plain bread, and vegetables. They need not expect to relish at first food so different from that which they have been indulging themselves to eat. If they cannot at first enjoy plain food, they should fast until they can. That fast will prove to them of greater benefit than medicine, for the abused stomach will find that rest which it has long needed, and real hunger can be satisfied with a plain diet. It will take time for the taste to recover from the abuses which it has received, and to gain its natural tone. But perseverance in a self-denying course of eating and drinking will soon make plain, wholesome food palatable, and it will soon be eaten with greater satisfaction than the epicure enjoys over his rich dainties."
Counsels on Diet and Foods, p. 190

GRAVIES

MUSHROOM GRAVY

⅓ cup cashews

1 cup hot, cooked rice or cooked garbanzos

2 Tbs. dried onions

1 Tbs. McKay's Chicken Seasoning

4 Tbs. Bragg's Liquid Aminos or 2 Tbs. soy sauce

½ tsp. garlic powder

3 Tbs. cornstarch

3½ cups water

1 - 4 oz. can mushrooms

1. Place all ingredients except mushrooms in blender with 2 cups of the water. Blend for at least one minute until smooth, adding remaining water at the end.

2. Place in a sauce pan with mushrooms and bring to a boil, stirring constantly. Add more water if needed to the desired consistency. Serve with potatoes, roasts, or patties.

EASY CHICKEN-LIKE GRAVY

2 cups water

½ medium onion

¾ cups garbanzos

¼ cup flour

½ tsp. salt

⅛ tsp. ground celery seed

4 Tbs. soy sauce or 1½ Tbs. McKay's Chicken Seasoning

1. Blend garbanzos in small amount of the water until smooth, then add the remaining ingredients (including the onion cut in pieces) and blend briefly.

2. Cook over low heat for 20 minutes, stirring frequently. Serve.

Prep. Time: 5 min.
Cooking time: 5 min.

BROWN GRAVY

Scant ½ cup unbleached flour

4 cups Cashew Milk (p. 20)

1 Tbs. Bragg's Liquid Aminos or soy sauce

1 rounded Tbs. McKay's Chicken Seasoning

½ tsp. garlic powder

1 tsp. onion powder

½ tsp. salt or more to taste

1. Place flour in a non-stick skillet over high heat and stir constantly until lightly browned. No oil or spray is needed on the pan for this.

2. Place liquid in blender; add seasonings and browned flour. Blend briefly.

3. Pour into sauce pan or non-stick skillet and bring to a boil, stirring constantly.

Prep. time: 15 min.
Cooking time: 15 min.

Makes 5 cups

Nutrient Information
Per Serving (½ cup)

CALORIES	58
PROTEIN	8%
FAT	35% / 2.2 gm
CARBOHYDRATE	57%
SODIUM	347 mg

Makes 3 cups

Nutrient Information
Per Serving (¼ cup)

CALORIES	67
PROTEIN	21%
FAT	9% / .7 gm
CARBOHYDRATE	70%
SODIUM	435 mg

Makes 4 cups

Nutrient Information
Per Serving (½ cup)

CALORIES	62
PROTEIN	11%
FAT	38% / 2.7 gm
CARBOHYDRATE	51%
SODIUM	310 mg

Toppings—Gravies and Sauces

SWEET-SOUR SAUCE

SWEET-SOUR SAUCE

1 cup soy sauce or Bragg's Liquid Aminos

½ cup conc. fruit sweetener or ⅓ cup honey

3½ cups water

¼ cup cornstarch dissolved in ½ cup water

Mix all together and stir while bringing to a boil. Serve over Tofu Walnut Balls or a stir-fry-type vegetable dish.

Prep. time: 5 min.
Cooking time: 5 min.

CREAM SAUCE

CREAM SAUCE

1 cup cooked rice

¾ cup cashew nuts

2 cups hot water

1 Tbs. McKay's Chicken Seasoning

1 tsp. salt

1 Tbs. onion powder

2 Tbs. cornstarch or 3 Tbs. white flour

2 cups water

1 tsp. basil, opt.

2 Tbs. dried chives, opt.

1. Blend rice and cashews in hot water for about 2 minutes until smooth.

2. While blending, add seasonings and cornstarch or flour.

3. Pour blended cashew mixture into a saucepan with the remaining 2 cups water, basil, and dried chives. Bring to a boil, stirring constantly.

Serving Tip: Very good as a cream sauce for vegeta-

THAI-PEANUT SAUCE

THAI PEANUT SAUCE

¼ cup peanut butter

1½ cups water

¼ cup Bragg's Liquid Aminos or soy sauce

2½ Tbs. molasses

1½ Tbs. cornstarch

2 tsp. lemon juice or tomato sauce

1. Place all ingredients in blender and blend smooth.

2. Pour into a saucepan and bring to a boil.

Serving tip: Serve with rice or quinoa and steamed vegetables.

Prep. time: 5 min.
Cooking time: 5 min.

Makes 5 cups

Nutrient Information
Per Serving (¼ cup)

CALORIES	28
PROTEIN	4%
FAT	0% / 0 gm
CARBOHYDRATE	96%
SODIUM	660 mg

Makes 5 cups

Nutrient Information
Per Serving (½ cup)

CALORIES	88
PROTEIN	9%
FAT	48% / 4.9 gm
CARBOHYDRATE	43%
SODIUM	263 mg

Makes 2 ¼ cups

Nutrient Information
Per Serving (¼ cup)

CALORIES	64
PROTEIN	12%
FAT	47% / 3.6 gm
CARBOHYDRATE	41%
SODIUM	378 mg

Toppings—Gravies and Sauces

Marinara Sauce

Pesto Sauce

MARINARA SAUCE

1 large onion, diced

½ cup diced green pepper

2 cups water

2 cups diced, canned tomatoes

1 cup tomato sauce

1 Tbs. Bragg's Liquid Aminos or soy sauce

1 tsp. salt

¾ tsp. paprika

1½ tsp. garlic powder or 2 cloves garlic

½ tsp. oregano

1 tsp. basil

½ tsp. cumin

¼ tsp. celery salt

⅛ tsp. each: thyme and marjoram (opt.)

2 Tbs. cornstarch

1. Simmer onion and green pepper in some of the water for 5 minutes.

2. Add remaining water and all remaining ingredients except cornstarch. Bring to a boil and simmer for 20 minutes.

3. Dissolve cornstarch in a small amount of water and slowly add to sauce while stirring to thicken.

PESTO SAUCE

1½ cups water

½ cup pine nuts*

½ cup cashew nuts*

1 Tbs. sesame tahini

2 Tbs. fresh lemon juice

1 cup fresh basil

½ cup fresh parsley

2 cloves garlic

1 Tbs. onion powder

1½ tsp. salt

1 - 2 Tbs. potato flour

Just about any nut may be substituted such as al-monds or walnuts, but this is a very good combination. Walnuts give it a distinc-tive flavor and a darker color, but are also a good choice.

1. Place all ingredients except potato flour in blender and blend until smooth.

2. Add potato flour a little at a time. This will thicken the sauce as it blends. Just add the amount needed to make the consistency you like for a sauce that can be spooned over spaghetti without being runny.

Tip: This sauce should not be heated. Cooking or even heating will change the fresh green color and taste. Serve over steaming hot spaghetti and marinara or pasta sauce, but notice that this sauce is rich and should not be used liberally, but as a flavor enhancer to make plain spaghetti more special.

Marinara Sauce Makes 6 cups

Nutrient Information
Per Serving (1 cup)

CALORIES	27
PROTEIN	13%
FAT	6% / .2 gm
CARBOHYDRATE	81%
SODIUM	270 mg

Pesto Sauce makes 2½ cups

Nutrient Information
Per Serving (¼ cup)

CALORIES	98
PROTEIN	13%
FAT	66% / 8 gm
CARBOHYDRATE	21%
SODIUM	323 mg

Toppings—Gravies and Sauces

CRANBERRY SAUCE

CRANBERRY SAUCE

¾ cup conc. grape juice

⅓ cup conc. orange juice

½ cup conc. apple juice

⅔ cup dates

1 - 12 oz. pkg. cranberries, fresh or frozen

1. Blend dates with grape juice, adding orange and apple juice a little at a time until very smoothly blended.

2. Add the cranberries and blend to desired consistency. If mix is too thin, Clear Jel may be added as needed for a thicker sauce. For a jellied sauce, boil one stick of agar (4 Tbs. flakes) in 1 cup water and simmer for 1 minute; blend into the mix and chill. Diversify this idea according to your taste using less or more sweet. You can use some water in place of juice or use apple juice in place of the grape.

Makes 4 cups

Nutrient Information
Per Serving (¼ cup)

CALORIES	76
PROTEIN	3%
FAT	2% / .1 gm
CARBOHYDRATE	95%
SODIUM	3 mg

SALSA

SALSA

2 large ripe tomatoes

⅓ of a bunch of fresh cilantro

1 large onion

½ of a fresh red bell pepper

½ tsp. salt

3 Tbs. lemon juice

1 tsp. paprika

¼ tsp. garlic powder

1. Pulse blend all ingredients until salsa consistency.

2. Chill and serve.

Note: Make sure you use tasty tomatoes—2 cups canned tomatoes can be used instead of fresh if desired.

Makes 24 servings

Nutrient Information
Per Serving (2 Tbs.)

CALORIES	8
PROTEIN	12%
FAT	7% / 0 gm
CARBOHYDRATE	81%
SODIUM	81 mg

BARBECUE SAUCE

BARBECUE SAUCE

3½ cups tomato puree

½ cup water

½ cup pineapple juice

½ cup conc. fruit sweetener or honey

3 Tbs. molasses

1 Tbs. lemon juice

¾ tsp. Wright's Hickory Seasoning

¼ cup Kitchen Bouquet

¼ tsp. onion powder

¼ tsp. garlic powder

⅛ tsp. cumin

2 tsp. salt

Mix together in a kettle, bring to a boil, and simmer for ½ hr.

Serve on Hickory Burgers (p. 55) or Grlled Tofu Slices (p. 52)

Prep. time: 10 min.
Cooking time: 30 min.

Makes 6 cups

Nutrient Information
Per Serving (¼ cup)

CALORIES	39
PROTEIN	7%
FAT	1% / 0 gm
CARBOHYDRATE	92%
SODIUM	271 mg

Toppings—Cheeses

We have included several cheese-like recipes in this section, some lower in fat than others. In our restaurant we find the higher-fat Tahini Cheese to be a favorite because it resembles real cheese the most in flavor and appearance. We include these recipes here with the caution that they be used more for entertaining and special occasions and not a part of the daily fare.

"Children are allowed to eat flesh meats, spices, butter, cheese, pork, rich pastry, and condiments generally. They are also allowed to eat irregularly and between meals of unhealthful food. These things do their work of deranging the stomach, exciting the nerves to unnatural action, and enfeebling the intellect. Parents do not realize that they are sowing the seed which will bring forth disease and death." *Counsels on Diet and Food,* p.369

Toppings—Cheeses

SLICEABLE CASHEW CHEESE

PARMESAN CHEESES

SLICEABLE CASHEW CHEESE
(White or Yellow)

2 cups cashew nuts

⅜ cup Emes Kosher Gel

1½ cups boiling water

2 Tbs. lemon juice

2 Tbs. yeast flakes

1 Tbs. salt

1 tsp. onion powder

½ tsp. garlic powder

1 cup cold water

1. Place all ingredients in the blender except the 1 cup cold water. Turn on and blend for 1 or 2 minutes until very smooth.

   Hint: Place a towel over the lid of the blender before turning on. Hot liquids tend to splash out.

2. Add 1 cup cold water, blend briefly and pour into containers of your choice to chill and slice when firm.

Hint: This recipe makes a white cheese resembling Jack cheese. If you want half of it to resemble American cheese in color, pour half of it into a 1 pint mold and blend in ¼ cup pimientos and 1 tsp. paprika to the remainder. This can be frozen, so you might want to make a double recipe and keep it handy for future use, Frozen Cashew Cheese shreds very nicely if you do it while still frozen, and makes a great topping for Pizza. To thaw, set out at room temperature for an hour. Don't try to thaw it in the microwave—it will melt and not be sliceable.

*Prep. time: 15 min.
Chilling time: 4 hr. or overnight*

NON-DAIRY PARMESAN CHEESE

½ cup yeast flakes

½ cup ground sesame seeds

2 tsp. garlic powder

1 tsp. onion powder

1 Tbs. chicken-like seasoning

1 Tbs. lemon juice

Mix together all ingredients and store in an air-tight container in the refrigerator.

Hint: The best way to grind sesame seeds is in a small, electric seed or coffee mill.

Prep. time: 10 min.

Makes 4 cups

Nutrient Information
Per Serving (2 Tbs.)
CALORIES	46
PROTEIN	11%
FAT	69% / 3.7 gm
CARBOHYDRATE	20%
SODIUM	203 mg

Makes 1 cups

Nutrient Information
Per Serving (1 Tbs.)
CALORIES	39
PROTEIN	23%
FAT	48% / 2.2 gm
CARBOHYDRATE	29%
SODIUM	5.5 mg

Toppings—Cheeses

TAHINI CHEESE

CHEESY SAUCE

TAHINI CHEESE

2 cups water

1 cup well cooked rice

½ cup cashew nuts

½ cup sesame tahini (Joyva brand is best)

3 Tbs. yeast flakes

1 Tbs. onion powder

¼ tsp. garlic powder

¼ tsp. dill (opt.)

¾ cup pimientos

2 Tbs. lemon juice

1½ tsp. Vege-Sal (or 1 tsp. salt)

¼ tsp. paprika

1-2 Tbs. potato flour (opt.)

Blend all ingredients until smooth. Potato flour may be added if thicker sauce is desired, but it thickens when cooked or broiled on toast.

Prep. time: 10 min.

CHEESY SAUCE VARIATION

This recipe is simpler (no corn starch, fewer ingredients) but richer

1 cup cashews

2 cups water

½ red bell pepper or ¼ cup pimentos

2 tsp. salt

1 tsp. onion powder

1 Tbs. yeast flakes, opt.

Directions: same as Cheesy Sauce

For a sliceable cheese, add add ⅓ cup Emes Kosher Gel to the blended mixture before boiling. Pour into a container and chill. May be shredded or sliced.

CHEESY SAUCE

½ cup cashew nuts

2 Tbs. sesame tahini (opt.)

3 cups water

1 Tbs. lemon juice

⅓ cup pimentos or diced red peppers (canned)

½ tsp. garlic powder

1 tsp. onion powder

1½ tsp. salt

2 Tbs. yeast flakes

2 ½ Tbs. cornstarch

1. Blend all ingredients until very smooth.

2. Place in a saucepan and bring to a boil while stirring.

Serving Tips: Serve hot over broccoli, cauliflower, or other vegetables. Or drizzle over tortilla chips for Nachos. Or fold into cooked macaroni (2 cups dry) for Macaroni and Cheese.

Makes 4 cups

Nutrient Information
Per Serving (2 Tbs.)

CALORIES	48
PROTEIN	12%
FAT	55% / 3 gm
CARBOHYDRATE	33%
SODIUM	107 mg

Makes 4 cups

Nutrient Information
Per Serving (½ cup)

CALORIES	53
PROTEIN	10%
FAT	64% / 4 gm
CARBOHYDRATE	26%
SODIUM	405 mg

CHEESE TOO

TOFU CHEESE*

CHEESE TOO

½ cup cashew nuts

1¼ cup fine cornmeal or corn flour

3 cups water

½ cup tomato sauce

3 tsp. onion powder

3 Tbs. dried onion flakes

1 tsp. garlic powder

1 tsp. lemon juice (or more to taste)

½ tsp. conc. orange juice

½ tsp. conc. apple juice

1 tsp. fructose or honey

1 tsp. paprika

3 Tbs. pimiento

3 Tbs. potato flour

1½ - 2 tsp. salt

1. Place cornmeal in a saucepan and stir in 2 cups of water. Bring to a boil and simmer for 10 minutes.

2. Place cooked cornmeal in blender with remaining ingredients and blend for about 2 minutes, taking the precaution to cover the lid with a dish towel when you first turn on the blender to protect from possible splashing when the blender first starts with a hot liquid inside.

3. Pour into a container and chill. It will set up and become quite thick, like cream cheese, when it cools

Variation: For a "cream cheese" color, omit the tomato sauce, paprika and pimientoes.

Prep. time: 10 min.

*Both these recipes are even lower in fat than those on the previous pages.

TOFU CHEESE

1¼ cups tofu

1 cup cooked quick oats (½ cup oats in ¾ cup water)

½ cup water

2 Tbs. dried onion flakes

2 Tbs. yeast flakes

¾ tsp. salt

¾ tsp. paprika

½ tsp. dill weed

1 tsp. conc. apple juice

1 tsp. orange juice

½ tsp. lemon juice

¼ cup pimiento

1 Tbs. thick tomato sauce

2 Tbs. potato flour

¼ tsp. Wright's Hickory Seasoning—add if desired

Place all in blender and blend until smooth. May be used as a sauce on vegetables or pizza or lasagna.

Prep. time: 15 min.

Makes 2½ cups

Nutrient Information

Per Serving (2 Tbs.)

CALORIES	129
PROTEIN	9%
FAT	27% / 3.7 gm
CARBOHYDRATE	64%
SODIUM	397 mg

Makes 2 cups

Nutrient Information

Per Serving (2 Tbs.)

CALORIES	93
PROTEIN	30%
FAT	34% / 3.8 gm
CARBOHYDRATE	36%
SODIUM	219 mg

BAKING

For centuries, bread has been a symbol of all that is good in life. It accompanies our simplest and most humble meals, and is present at our most festive occasions.

Fruit Bread Wreath (p. 124), tarts with strawberry filling (p. 11) and Blueberry Sauce (p. 7)

"It requires thought and care to make good bread. But there is more religion in a good loaf of bread than many think."
E. G. White, *Counsels on Diet and Foods*, p. 316

Baking—Yeast Raised Bread

GENERAL INSTRUCTIONS

YEAST BREADS

Bread is, indeed, the staff of life. Jesus said, "I am the bread of life," (John 6:38) comparing our need for spiritual food to our basic need for bread.

Much of the bread people buy or spend their labor on has been robbed of its value—in vitamins, minerals, and fiber—driving home the ironic question in Isaiah 55:2, "Wherefore do ye spend money for that which is not bread? and your labour for that which satisfieth not? Hearken diligently unto me, and eat ye that which is good, and let your soul delight itself in fatness." Could Jesus have been looking forward to our time when He bid us pray, "Give us this day our daily bread?" *Matthew* 6:11

Even most of the whole wheat flour that is available in stores is degerminated to give it a longer shelf life, but robbing the grain of much of its nutritive value. For this reason, we recommend that you purchase a flour mill, if at all possible, and grind your own grain. This is an investment that will come back to you many times over in the years to come. Many meals may be prepared with some type of bread as the entree. It might be pocket bread, pizza, bagels, burgers, bread dressing, french toast, fruit toast and so on! Bread making is exciting, never losing its charm. Children love to work with it and many a father or son cannot resist the fascination of making bread.

Bread needs to be light, well-baked to stop the yeast action, and eaten in abundance. To avoid eating fresh yeast, it is best to wait a day or two before eating the sliced delicacy. Toasted bread and particularly zwieback are easily digested. "Bread which is two or three days old is more healthful than new bread. Bread dried in the oven is one of the most wholesome articles of diet." *Counsels on Diet and Foods*, p. 317.

GENERAL BREAD MAKING DIRECTIONS

Utensils: Large mixing bowl or bread mixer, large heavy-handled spoon, measuring cups and spoons, sharp knife, rubber spatula, timer, thermometer, and bread pans. A bread scale is also very helpful for making uniform loaves.

Preparing pans: Teflon or Silverstone pans usually need no greasing and are excellent to use. If some greasing is necessary, a spray-on pan coating works very well.

Shaping: Cut dough into sizes needed to fill pans about ⅔ full for lovely high-domed bread. If you have a scale, you can weigh each ball of dough for uniform sizes. After doing this a few times you will learn just what weight is best for your pans and it will take out all the guesswork. Normal bread pans take about 1 to 1½ lbs. each. Knead each piece of dough into a tight ball and then stretch or roll into a rectangle. Starting

Baking—Yeast Raised Bread

on the long side, roll the rectangle tightly and turn down each end toward the seam. Place in the pan with the seam side down. The top should be smooth and rounded. Do not press down into the pan.

@BODY BREAD = Pineapple or tomato juice cans are excellent for making round loaves. Just knead dough into a tight ball and drop into sprayed can with smooth side up—the can should be half full. Let rise upright until dough rises to the top of the can.

Rising: Read each of the methods listed below and choose.

1. (25-30 min.) Preheat oven to 200° and TURN OFF. Place loaves in oven and close door until bread has doubled in size. Test by pressing finger gently into side of loaf. Indentation will remain when sufficiently risen. Remove the loaves gently and preheat oven to baking temperature, then return loaves to oven.

2. (30-45 min.) Place loaves in a warm room (about 80-90°) and cover with a wet cloth that does not touch dough. Bake in preheated oven when doubled.

3. (15-20 min.) Place covered loaves on rack over hot water in sink, or on heating pad which is covered with a bath towel and set on medium heat.

4. (45 min.- 1 hr. or more) Place loaves on kitchen counter and let rise at room temperature, or even in the refrigerator and allow to rise slowly. Slow rising gives bread a finer texture.

Baking: Choose the most convenient. Preheat oven.

1. Bake at 400° for 30 minutes—crisp crust.

2. Bake at 350° for 45 minutes—soft crust.

3. Bake at 400° for ten minutes, then lower to 350° for 30 minutes.

Bread is finished baking when it is brown on top, slightly brown on sides and sounds hollow upon tapping side. When baking is complete, remove to cooling racks. When cool, store in plastic bags and freeze extra loaves.

Trouble shooting:

Flat tops indicate too moist dough (should have added more flour) or undeveloped gluten (should have kneaded longer). Cracked sides indicate too much flour, or too rapid rising or fast baking.

Small, heavy loaves usually are the result of poor quality flour (not enough gluten content) and/or too much flour (dry, stiff dough).

Don't underestimate the value of good, high-gluten flour. I have found that when I am having consistently poor bread, the problems can all disappear with a good batch of high-gluten wheat. Then, whatever I do, it seems the result is beautiful! Check with a health food co-op, or a store that sells kitchen flour mills, and ask for their best hard wheat. The gluten content should be 16-17%. Adding a half cup of gluten flour or Do-pep helps, but still never quite matches the quality of good hard wheat!

Baking—Yeast Raised Bread

WHOLE WHEAT BREAD

5 cups hot water (115°)

⅔ cups conc. apple juice or ¾ cup barley malt or ½ cup honey

1 cup applesauce or 2 medium apples, cored and grated or blended with some of the water

3 Tbs. dry yeast

1½ Tbs. salt

⅓ cup gluten flour or Do-pep

12-15 cups whole wheat flour

MIXER METHOD

1. Place hot water, apple juice or sweetener and applesauce in mixer bowl; add 7 cups of flour and ⅓ cup gluten flour.

Start mixer and sprinkle in the yeast; mix for 2 minutes. Turn off and scrape the sides, cover and let rise to the top of the bowl— about 15 minutes.

Hint: Raising the dough first in this soft sponge stage allows the gluten to develop before adding the rest of the flour, giving the bread a better texture—less flour will be needed in the second mixing.

Makes 4-5 loaves, 10 slices each

Nutrient Information
Per Serving (1 slice)
CALORIES	124
PROTEIN	15%
FAT	5% / .7 gm
CARBOHYDRATE	80%
SODIUM	194 mg

2. Turn on the mixer to beat down the raised sponge, and add the salt. At this point other ingredients may be added to create special breads such as raisins, dates, nuts, or dried vegetables. While mixer is turning, add remaining flour gradually until dough begins to pull away from the sides of the bowl. Mix for 10 minutes. If flour is sufficient in amount the sides of the bowl should be clean in six minutes.

3. Remove from mixer to a lightly floured or oiled surface–shape into loaves; follow directions for shaping, raising, and baking.

HAND METHOD

1. Place hot water, apple juice or sweetener, and applesauce in a large mixing bowl, sprinkle yeast over the liquid and add 7 cups of flour and ⅓ cup gluten flour, beating with a sturdy spoon to mix into batter. Beat rhythmically for 3 minutes, cover and let rise until double– about 15-20 minutes.

2. Add the salt and any other special additions such as raisins, dates, nuts, or dried vegetables of your choice. Add as much flour as can be beaten vigorously by hand for 6 minutes.

Next, mix in as much of the flour as can be managed (when mixing by hand, more flour is added progressively but enough needs to be added at this time to make a mix "dry" enough to remove from the bowl onto a floured surface or board). Cover and let rest for 10 minutes.

3. Knead gently and rhythmically for 30 minutes. Keep dough covered with a light sheaf of flour. Do not press through this sheaf as you knead. Well-developed gluten takes up flour slowly, preventing dough from becoming too dry. Keep hands well floured, but add flour gradually on board. If hands and board become sticky or coated, scrape up with a metal spatula, clean hands and start again.

4. Time's up! Cover and let rest 10 minutes. Follow directions for shaping, rising, and baking.

WHOLE WHEAT VARIATIONS

Raisin Bread—Add 3 cups raisins in step #2.

Papaya—Add 2½ cups diced, dried papaya in step #2

Apricot-Almond—Add 2 cups diced dried apricots and 1½ cups coarsely chopped almonds in step #2

110

Baking—Yeast Raised Bread

Oat-bran Sunflower Seed —Add 2 cups sunflower seeds and 1 cup oat bran in step #2

Pumpkin-Orange-Raisin — Substitute orange juice concentrate for apple juice concentrate, cooked pumpkin or winter squash for applesauce and add 2-3 cups raisins in step #2. For more orange flavor, add finely grated rind of ½ orange.

Vegetable—Substitute 2 cups carrot juice for 2 cups of the water, or blend 1 large carrot into some of the hot water until smooth. Then add ¾ cups dried vegetable flakes and ½ cup dried onion flakes in step #2.

Potato—Substitute 2 cups cooked potatoes for applesauce. Mash or blend with some of the water before adding in step #1.

Multi-Grain—Replace up to 2 cups of whole wheat flour with barley, rye, corn, kamut, or triticale flours. Limit to two or three varieties since grains low in gluten will tend to make the bread heavier. To make multi-grain breads lighter, bakers usually use some white flour.

SPROUTED WHOLE WHEAT

4 cups whole wheat soaked in 3 cups water for 36 hrs.

1 cup conc. apple juice

3 cups hot water

2½ Tbs. yeast

1½ Tbs. salt

10-12 cups whole wheat flour

1. Place 4 cups wheat covered with 3 cups water in a covered bowl, and keep at room temperature. Stir three times a day. Each 12 hours, drain and rinse, leaving them in about ½ cup water. Grains will not actually sprout, but will partially burst!

2. Grind the wheat in an old-fashioned meat grinder on fine. Or place in blender, 2 cups at a time with the hot water and apple juice in this recipe, and blend fine. A food processor also works for this.

3. Place ground wheat in mixing bowl along with the water and juice. Add yeast and 2 cups of the whole wheat flour.

MIXER METHOD

1. Mix for 2 minutes; cover and let rise to top of bowl—about 15 minutes.

2. Add salt and 8 cups of flour gradually while mixer is running. Within 6 minutes the mix should pull away from the sides. Add another cup of flour if needed, but do not make too dry. Mix ten minutes for this step. Remove from mixer and shape into loaves, raise and bake.

HAND METHOD

1. Beat with a large spoon for 7 minutes. Cover and let double.

2. Add salt and enough flour to be able to mix and remove to a floured surface. Cover and let rest 10 minutes.

3. Knead gently and rhythmically for 30 minutes. Kneading is fun and healthful. Listen to a tape or listen to some nice music. Cover and let rest 10 minutes.

4. Shape into loaves, raise, and bake.

Makes
Nutrient Information
Per Serving (1 slice)

CALORIES	111
PROTEIN	14%
FAT	5% / .6 gm
CARBOHYDRATE	81%
SODIUM	162 mg

POCKET (PITA) BREAD

1 Recipe Whole Wheat
Bread dough (p. 110)

1 cup or more cornmeal

1 cup or more sesame seeds

1. The best way to bake Pocket Bread is on quarry tile which may be purchased at any floor covering store. You will need about 3 - 12" tiles, or more if they are smaller. Place them on the lowest possible rack of your oven and preheat to 500°.

2. Prepare your table for cutting and rolling the dough. It is helpful to have plenty of space for this. You will need several cookie sheets, depending on how many pockets you want to make. (You probably won't want to make the whole batch into Pocket Bread, so the remainder of the dough can be made into bread.) Have a rolling pin ready and place the cornmeal and sesame seeds each in separate bowls for dipping.

---

1 loaf makes 8 large pitas

Nutrient Information
Per Serving (1 pita)
CALORIES	100
PROTEIN	15%
FAT	5% / .7 gm
CARBOHYDRATE	80%
SODIUM	194 mg

1. Make Whole Wheat Bread dough. When it is ready to form into loaves, take a piece of dough and roll into a rope about 2½ inches in diameter. Cut into pieces and roll each into a 2-inch ball. This can vary according to the size you wish.

2. As each ball is made, dip the bottom firmly into the cornmeal and the top into the sesame seeds. Place cornmeal side down on the table to rest as you form the other balls.

3. Starting with the first ball that was formed, flatten with your hand, cornmeal side down, and roll from center out until it is ¼ inch thick. Place on an upside down cookie sheet which has been sprinkled with cornmeal and let rise at room temperature for 15 minutes.

4. With a large metal spatula, gently but quickly slip two or three pitas onto the hot tile. Once it touches the tile there is no moving it, so aim carefully! Practice makes perfect.

5. Bake about 4 minutes. Around a minute after they hit the hot tile, they will puff up like a balloon, forming the "pocket." Watch carefully—they burn easily.

6. Remove and place on cooling rack and repeat with next pockets until all are baked and cooling.

7. For smaller pita, cut about half way around the edge of the circle (to make an opening). Larger ones may be cut in half across the center forming 2 half-circle pitas. Place in plastic bags as soon as they are cool and freeze any extra to keep them fresh.

Note: 1 whole bread recipe will make a lot of pita! Use some of your recipe for pita and the rest for loaves.

Baking—Yeast Raised Bread

OLD WORLD RYE

PARTY RYE

OLD WORLD RYE

1½ cups warm water

2 Tbs. dry yeast

1 Tbs. molasses

2 Tbs. caraway seeds

2 tsp. salt

¼ cup carob powder

2 cups rye flour

2½ cups whole wheat flour

1. Dissolve yeast in ½ cup warm water. Combine rye flour and carob powder.

2. Combine molasses with remaining cup water. In large bowl, add salt and caraway seed, rye and carob mixture, ½ cup flour and yeast mixture.

3. Beat with spoon 7 minutes until dough is smooth. Spread remaining flour on a working surface and scrape soft dough onto this thick layer of flour. Knead flour into the dough adding more if necessary to make dough smooth and elastic (not sticky). Place in a bowl and raise.

4. Punch down dough when double in size. Shape into two small or one one large loaf. Place on a cookie sheet sprinkled with cornmeal and raise.

5. Bake at 375° for 35-40 minutes. Small loaves need only 30 minutes.

PARTY RYE

3 cups hot water

½ cup conc. apple juice

3 Tbs. dry yeast

1 Tbs. salt

2½ cups rye flour

6-8 cups whole wheat flour

½ cup gluten flour or Do-pep

2½ Tbs. caraway seeds

½ cup dehydrated onions

1. Combine water and apple juice and place all but 1 cup of this liquid in a large mixing bowl. Place remaining cup of water and apple juice mixture in a small bowl and sprinkle yeast "on" the liquid so it will dissolve.

2. While yeast is activating, begin mixing 3½ cups whole wheat flour into the liquid and either beat with a spoon or mix 5 minutes in a mixer.

3. Add yeast mixture and another cup of flour and continue beating or mixing in a soft stage for 3 minutes. Let rise for 30 minutes.

4. Add salt, caraway seeds, onions, gluten flour, rye flour, and additional whole wheat flour as needed to knead by hand or to pull away from sides of mixer bowl. Knead by mixer for 10 minutes, or by hand for 30 minutes.

5. Shape into small loaves, or shape into foot long "ropes" 2½ inches in diameter and place on a cookie sheet. Place far enough apart that they will not touch each other when rising. Let rise until double.

6. Bake at 425° for 10 minutes, reduce heat to 350° and bake about 20 minutes or until done.

Makes 2 loaves

Nutrient Information
Per Serving (1 slice)

CALORIES	103
PROTEIN	17%
FAT	6% / .7 gm
CARBOHYDRATE	77%
SODIUM	215 mg

Makes 4 - 6 small loaves

Nutrient Information
Per Serving (2 slices)

CALORIES	81
PROTEIN	17%
FAT	5% / .6 gm
CARBOHYDRATE	78%
SODIUM	321 mg

Baking—Yeast Raised Bread

BARLEY BUNS

BAGELS

BARLEY BUNS

2 cups warm water

2 Tbs. honey

2 tsp. salt

4 cups barley flour

1 cup white flour (for wheat free, just add extra barley flour)

2 Tbs. yeast

1. Dissolve yeast in ½ cup of the water. Put remaining water in a large mixing bowl. Add half of the barley flour and all the white flour and beat vigorously. Add honey, salt, and softened yeast and beat briskly, adding remaining flour in the amount needed to make dough that can be kneaded.

2. Place on a floured board. Knead until smooth and elastic. Shape into round, 2-inch balls and roll* into circles about ¼ inch thick. Place on a sprayed cookie sheet and let rise until double in size.

3. Bake at 350° for approximately 20 minutes.

*If you wish, spread a thick layer of sesame seeds on work area and before rolling buns, press the tops of the buns onto the seeds making the desired amount "stick" into the dough. Rolling after this step will press the seeds into the dough for a delightful sesame seed-topped barley bun.

Note: When our girls were little, they wanted me to make these all the time. We thought they resembled the pictures we had seen of "Little Lad" who shared his five barley loaves with Jesus and ultimately the multitude!

BAGELS

Any bread recipe can be made into Bagels. When bread is ready to shape into loaves, make some of it into Bagels as follows:

1. Roll the dough into a rope 2 inches in diameter and cut into pieces about the size of tennis balls. Roll each piece into a round ball that is as smooth and seamless as possible, and poke your index finger through the center. Twirl around your finger until it stretches into a ring with a hole in the middle. Allow to rise on a liberally sprayed cookie sheet until doubled.

2. While waiting, place 3½ quarts of water in a kettle with 1 Tbs. salt and bring to a boil.

3. Gently but quickly slip a thin, metal spatula under the Bagels and place in the boiling water for three minutes, turning rolls by pressing down on one side every 20 seconds. Do not attempt to place more than 4 or 5 in the kettle at one time.

4. Using a slotted spoon, remove from the water and place on a sprayed cookie tin. Bake at 425° for about 20-25 minutes until crust is browned. Cool on a rack.

Makes 12 Barley Buns

Nutrient Information
Per Serving (1 bun)

CALORIES	294
PROTEIN	11%
FAT	3% / .8 gm
CARBOHYDRATE	86%
SODIUM	360 mg

114

Baking—Yeast Raised Bread

LEFSE

LEFSE

3 Tbs. potato flour

¾ cups water

¼ tsp. salt

½ cup whole wheat flour

½ cup unbleached white flour

1. Put potato flour in mixing bowl. Gradually stir in the water.

2. Mix in separate bowl the flours and salt. Add to potato flour and water mixture.

3. Knead briefly on a well-floured board. Divide into 12 balls.

4. Roll each on a well floured board into a large, thin pancake and cook about 2 minutes on each side on a preheated non-stick skillet. Stack between two towels in a basket or platter until ready to serve.

Serving tip: These make delicious tortillas filled with Burrito fillings, or just eat as unleavened bread with any spread of your choice. We like to spread with peanut butter and creamed honey, rolled up for a dessert. Also good with Millet Butter.

WHOLE WHEAT TORTILLAS

WHOLE WHEAT TORTILLAS

2 cups water

1 cup rolled oats

¼ cup sesame seeds or 2 Tbs. tahini

½ tsp. salt

2 cups unbleached flour

2 cups whole wheat pastry flour

1. Blend first 4 ingredients until smooth. Pour into a bowl, add flour and knead briefly.

2. Roll each on a well floured board into a large, thin pancake and cook about 2 minutes on each side on a preheated non-stick skillet. Stack between two towels in a basket or platter until ready to serve.

Makes 12 servings

Nutrient Information

Per Serving

CALORIES	42
PROTEIN	13%
FAT	3% / .1 gm
CARBOHYDRATE	84%
SODIUM	90 mg

Makes 12 tortillas

Nutrient Information

Per Serving (1 tortilla)

CALORIES	172
PROTEIN	13%
FAT	12% / 2.3 gm
CARBOHYDRATE	75%
SODIUM	91 mg

Baking—Muffins and Quick Breads

Our muffins are very simple to make, using simple ingredients. They are very low in fat, too. Most of them are made with a blend of flours other than wheat. We did this to please the many people who come to us who are allergic to wheat, but we found this blend of flours to be very delightful in texture and taste. For all of us, a variety of grains in the diet is more desirable than one or two being used day after day. The leavening product we use is calcium carbonate with citric acid (Ener-G Baking Powder—see appendix for information on where to purchase).

Blueberry and Bran Muffins

"All wheat flour is not best for a continuous diet. A mixture of wheat, oatmeal, and rye would be more nutritious than the wheat with the nutrifying properties separated from it."
Counsels on Diet and Foods, p. 320

BLUEBERRY MUFFINS

1 cup applesauce

½ cup fruit juice sweetener (or ⅓ cup honey plus 2 Tbs. water)

½ cup water

2 cups blueberries (or use 1½ cups whole fresh or frozen raspberries, or blackberries)

3 cups whole grain flour such as barley, oat, or whole wheat pastry flour

3 Tbs. Ener-G Baking Powder*

1 tsp. salt

*May substitute 1½ Tbs. Rumford or other non-aluminum baking powder—See appendix on baking powder for how to order Ener-G products.

1. Place flour, baking powder and salt in a bowl and stir in the frozen (unthawed) blueberries. (May use fresh if you have them!)

2. Mix applesauce and fruit juice sweetener or honey together in a separate bowl, and stir into the dry mix.

3. Scoop into oiled or non-stick muffin tins.

Hint: A ½ cup ice cream scoop works great! The batter should be moist, but quite thick and able to hold its shape. If it seems too runny, just add more flour.

4. Bake 30 minutes at 325°, or until golden brown on top.

Hint: If using Ener-G Baking Powder (calcium carbonate), it is important to get the muffin tins into the pre-heated oven as soon as they are filled. This is a single-acting powder and the rising begins to take place as soon as they are mixed. Also we have found that the quality of the muffins is better if placed near the top of the oven with no other items in the oven above them.

Prep. time: 15 min.
Baking time: 30 min.

Hint: The secret to making perfect muffins lies in knowing just how moist to make your batter. Because of certain unpredictable variables such as flour texture and the moisture of fruits or applesauce, it is difficult to make a fool-proof recipe. If your muffins don't turn out perfect the first time, keep practicing and you will soon learn the art. Meanwhile, here are some clues that may help you. When adding the liquid or water, don't add it all at once. Reserve some of the water to add or leave out depending on the appearance of your batter. It should be soft and moist, but stiff enough to hold its shape when scooped into the muffin pan. If the batter is too wet, the muffins will rise and then fall during baking and look like a flat-topped mushroom. If the batter is too dry, the result will be heavy muffins that don't rise very much.

Makes 8 muffins

Nutrient Information
Per Serving (1 muffin)

CALORIES	118
PROTEIN	3%
FAT	3% / .5 gm
CARBOHYDRATE	94 %

BANANA NUT MUFFINS

3 cups whole grain flour such as barley, oat, or whole wheat pastry flour

3 Tbs. Ener-G Baking Powder*

1 tsp. salt

1½ cups water or for a richer result replace water with soy or Nut Milk

2 cups mashed ripe bananas

½ cup fruit juice sweetener, or ⅓ cup honey plus 2 Tbs. water

1 Tbs. vanilla

¼ tsp. maple flavoring

½ cup chopped walnuts, plus more to sprinkle on top

May substitute 1½ Tbs. Rumford or other non-aluminum baking powder—See appendix on baking powder for how to order Ener-G Foods.

1. Place flour, baking powder and salt in a bowl and mix together.

2. In a separate bowl, mix together the remaining ingredients and then stir in the dry mix.

3. Spoon into muffin tins (a ½ cup ice cream scoop is great for this), and sprinkle top with chopped walnuts.

4. Bake at 325° for 30 minutes, or until top is golden brown and center is done.

*Prep. time: 15 min.
Baking time: 30 min.*

STRAWBERRY BANANA MUFFINS

Same only replace walnuts with 1 cup finely chopped fresh or frozen strawberries.

Hint: A food processor makes it easy. Chop frozen berries while still partially frozen!

Makes 8 muffins

Nutrient Information
Per Serving (1 muffin)

CALORIES	328
PROTEIN	10%
FAT	16% / 6.2 gm
CARBOHYDRATE	74%
SODIUM	247 mg

HAWAIIAN MUFFINS

4 cups flour (1 cup each barley, oat, whole wheat pastry and white)

1½ cups unsweetened flaked coconut

3 Tbs. Ener-G Baking Powder (or 1½ Tbs. Rumford or similar baking powder)

1¼ tsp. salt

1 cup fructose

2 cups unsweetened pineapple chunks with juice

1. Mix together flours, coconut, baking powder and salt.

2. Mash pineapple chunks in a separate bowl and add to the flour mixture along with juice and fructose.

3. Beat with a large spoon, adding a bit more juice or water if needed to make a thick batter that will hold its shape and is not runny.

4. Spoon or scoop with a ½ cup ice cream scoop into oiled muffin tins.

5. Bake at 350° for about 30 minutes until browned and not gummy inside.

Prep. time: 15 min.
Baking time: 30 min.

Makes 10 muffins

Nutrient Information
Per Serving (1 muffin)

CALORIES	230
PROTEIN	9%
FAT	3% / .7 gm
CARBOHYDRATE	88%
SODIUM	245 mg

PUMPKIN MUFFINS

RAISIN-BRAN MUFFINS

PUMPKIN MUFFINS

3 cups whole grain flour such as barley, oat, or whole wheat pastry

3 Tbs. Ener-G Baking Powder (may substitute 1½ Tbs. Rumford or other non-aluminum baking powder—See appendix)

1 tsp. salt

1 tsp. coriander

½ tsp. cardamom

1 cup or more raisins

⅓ cup chopped walnuts

1 cup cooked or canned pumpkin (may use yams or squash)

1 Tbs. molasses

¼ tsp. maple flavoring

2 tsp. vanilla

¾ cup fruit juice sweetener or Date Sweetener (p. 130)

1½ cups Soy or Nut Milk

1. Place dry ingredients in a bowl (first 7 ingredients), and mix together.

2. Add remaining ingredients and beat together with a spoon until well mixed.

3. Spoon into muffin tins (a ½ cup ice cream scoop works great for this). Bake at 325° for 30 minutes.

Prep. time: 15 min.
Baking time: 30 min.

Makes 8 muffins

Nutrient Information
Per Serving (1 muffin)

CALORIES	328
PROTEIN	10%
FAT	10% / 4 gm
CARBOHYDRATE	80%
SODIUM	248 mg

RAISIN-BRAN MUFFINS

1½ cups whole wheat flour

1 cup unbleached flour

½ cup wheat or oat bran

3 Tbs. Ener-G Baking Powder

1 tsp. salt

2 cups raisins

1 cup applesauce

¾ cup Date Sweetener (p. 110)

1¼ cups water or soymilk

1. Mix together flours, bran, baking powder, salt and raisins.

2. Add remaining ingredients and mix well.

3. Spoon into muffin tins (a ½ cup ice cream scoop works great for this), and bake at 325° for 30 minutes.

Prep. time: 15 min.
Baking time: 30 min.

Makes 8 muffins

Nutrient Information
Per Serving (1 muffin)

CALORIES	285
PROTEIN	7%
FAT	2% / .7 gm
CARBOHYDRATE	91%
SODIUM	246 mg

CORN BREAD

QUICK FRUIT COBBLER

CORN BREAD

½ cup tofu

¾ cup water

½ cup applesauce

2 Tbs. fructose or honey

¾ cups cornmeal

¾ cups corn flour

½ cups whole wheat pastry flour or unbleached white flour

1 tsp. salt

1½ Tbs. Ener-G baking powder (or 1Tbs. Rumford)

1. Blend tofu with water and honey until smooth.

2. Place in mixing bowl along with applesauce. Stir in the remaining ingredients and stir briskly. It will be stiff compared to average cornbread, more like drop biscuits.

3. Spread into a 6 x 10 pan, or scoop into muffin tins. Bake at 375° for 20-30 minutes.

QUICK FRUIT COBBLER

The cobbler crust used in our Yeast Pastries section is a very tender and delicious yeast-raised crust. But since opening the Deli we have been using this quicker-to-make version which uses baking powder.

6 cups hot fruit filling (see recipes, p. 7)

½ cup water

⅓ cup applesauce

¼ cup fruit sweetener, Date Sweetener (p. 130), or honey

1 tsp. vanilla

1½ cups flour (may use whole wheat pastry, unbleached white, or barley or oat flour)

1 scant Tbs. Ener-G Baking Powder (or 1½ tsp. Rumford)

½ tsp. salt

1. Make the hot fruit filling and pour into an 8 x 8 inch baking dish.

2. In a small bowl, stir together the water, applesauce, fruit sweetener, and vanilla.

3. Stir in the flours, baking powder and salt; beat briskly with a spoon until well mixed.

4. Spread crust batter over hot fruit filling with a rubber spatula.

Hint: It is important that the fruit filling be hot in order for the crust to bake evenly on top and bottom. If desired, sprinkle top of cobbler crust with equal parts of coconut and walnuts (finely ground in a seed mill or blender) before baking. Or just sprinkle with sliced almonds or chopped walnuts and coconut.

5. Place immediately in oven at 350° and bake for about 30 minutes until crust is golden brown.

Prep. time: 20 min.
Cooking time: 30 min.

Makes 8 servings

Nutrient Information
Per Serving
CALORIES	176
PROTEIN	10%
FAT	18% / 3.7 gm
CARBOHYDRATE	72%
SODIUM	179 mg

Makes 9 servings

Nutrient Information
Per Serving
CALORIES	186
PROTEIN	8%
FAT	5% / 1 gm
CARBOHYDRATE	87%
SODIUM	136 mg

BAKING

Nothing quite compares to the aroma and eye appeal of freshly baked yeast breads. Whether you choose a loaf or a special shape, homemade yeast bread is fun to make and a great way to treat your family to a bit of wholesome goodness.

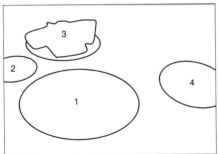

Photo key:

1. **Fruit Pizza**
2. **Blueberry Cobbler**
3. **Bear Claw**
4. **Fruit Bread Wreath**

FRUIT PIZZA

Here is a beautiful, appealing, special occasion dessert that everyone loves. This is such a favorite that we even served it instead of cake at our daughter's wedding!

1 recipe **Cashew Cheesecake (p. 152)** *

1 recipe **Basic Pastry Dough (p. 124)**

Sliced fresh strawberries, kiwi, and bananas, or other fruit in season

1 small can mandarin oranges

1 cup crushed pineapple

1 or 2 bananas

Finely shredded coconut

1. Make Cashew Cheesecake filling and pour into a container— chill until firm (about 2 hours).

> *If you want to speed up the chilling time, pour into a large, shallow metal baking dish and place in refrigerator.*

2. Make Basic Pastry Dough and divide into two balls. Roll each into a circle about the size of a pizza pan. Stretch onto two 12 inch non-stick or oiled pizza pans and flute the edges; prick with fork. Let rise in a warm place about 30 minutes. Bake at 400° for 7 or 8 minutes, or until golden brown.

3. Spoon chilled filling into a blender and blend smooth.

> *Hint: You will need to help the blending process by scraping the sides of the blender with a rubber spatula, helping the unblended portion toward the middle and into the blades.*

4. Pour filling onto 2 crusts and spread evenly over the surface with spatula.

5. Arrange sliced fruits on top, making a kaleidoscope of color according to fruits in season.

> *Hint: Don't try to use any plain frozen fruits such as blueberries or strawberries since the juice bleeds off as they melt and looks messy. If fresh strawberries aren't available, you can use a thickened, cooled fruit sauce (especially nice using Clear Jel) along with other fresh sliced fruits.*

Prep. time: 60 min.
Baking time: 40 min.
(Includes rising time)
Takes 2 hr. to chill.

Vanilla Pudding (p. 154) is also very good for a filling. Pour hot pudding directly onto Pizza Crust and chill before arranging fruits on top.

Makes 2 - 12″ pizzas

Nutrient Information
Per Serving 1/8 of pizza

CALORIES	200
PROTEIN	8%
FAT	35% / 8.2 gm
CARBOHYDRATE	57%
SODIUM	261 mg

FRUIT BREAD WREATH*

BASIC DOUGH

FRUIT BREAD WREATH

Double recipe of Basic Pastry Dough (p. 124)

2 cups diced dried fruit—raisins, currents, papaya, pineapple

1½ cups chopped walnuts or pecans

1. Place pastry dough on a floured surface and knead lightly for about 5 minutes.

2. Roll out into a long rectangle and apply a thin layer of Date Spread on the top surface (see next page). Sprinkle evenly with dried fruits and chopped nuts.

3. Roll up the long way (like a jelly roll) and pinch the seam closed. Transfer to a large non-stick baking sheet, seam down. Bring ends of this "tube" or roll together to form a circle, and pinch this seam closed. Flatten the ring slightly to about half the height.

4. With scissors make cuts from the outer edge toward the center of the circle about ¾ of the way through the dough, spacing the cuts about 1 inch apart.

5. *Every other* one of these pieces (made by the cuts) will be "flopped over" to the inside of the circle—grasp a piece on the outer edge of the circle, lift it up and over toward the center of the circle and quarter-twist it so that the date mixture is "showing" face up.

6. The pieces still pointing outward are not moved except to be quarter-twisted in place like the others. Repeat all the way around the circle.

7. Let rise in a warm place 15 - 20 minutes. Bake at 350° for 45 minutes or until done. Brush with fruit juice sweetener after removing from the oven.

Prep. time: 1 hr. 30 min.
Baking time: 45 min.

*Courtesy of
Rilla Klingbeil

BASIC PASTRY DOUGH

½ Tbs. yeast

⅓ cup warm water

1 Tbs. apple juice conc.

½ cup cashews

⅔ cup warm water

1 cup whole wheat flour

1 cup unbleached flour

1 tsp. salt

1. Place the ⅓ cup warm water in a small bowl and add the apple juice conc. and yeast. Let sit for 5 minutes.

2. Blend cashews and water in blender until smooth. Place in bowl with dissolved yeast.

3. Stir in the flours and salt; place on board and knead lightly. If dough is too sticky to knead, add more flour, but it should be soft like a Bisquick dough.

4. Use as noted in Fruit Cobbler, Fruit Bread Wreath, Bear Claws and Fruit Pizza.

Makes delicious biscuits

Prep. time: 60 min.
Baking time: 30 min.

Makes 20 servings

Nutrient Information
Per Serving

CALORIES	289
PROTEIN	9%
FAT	26% / 9 gm
CARBOHYDRATE	65%
SODIUM	245 mg

Fruit Bread Wreath, Bearclaws

Step #1-2

Step #3

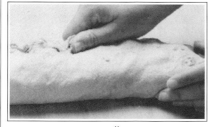

Step #3

Step #3

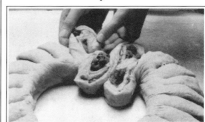

Step #4

Step #5 - 6

Step # 6

Bearclaw Step #1 - 2

Bearclaws: Applying Date Spread, cut into sections, cutting "claws" about half way through.

Baking—Yeast Pastries

FRUIT COBBLER

FRUIT COBBLER

½ recipe of Basic Pastry
Dough (p. 124)

6 cups Hot Thickened
Fruit Sauce (See recipe)

1. Place Hot Fruit Sauce
in 8-inch square or 9-inch
round baking dish.

2. Roll out Pastry Dough
to about ½ inch thick.

3. Carefully place dough
on top of hot fruit and
prick with a fork in several
places to let the steam
escape.

4. Let rise for 20 minutes,
then place in preheated
350° oven and bake
about 30 minutes, or
until golden brown.

*Hint: Make a whole recipe
of Basic Pastry Dough, using
half for cobbler and making
the other half into a pizza
crust. Pre-bake and freeze
for future use.*

*Prep. time: 45 min.
(Includes rising time)
Baking time: 30 min.*

Makes 8 servings

Nutrient Information
Per Serving

CALORIES	274
PROTEIN	5%
FAT	10% /3 gm
CARBOHYDRATE	85%
SODIUM	153 mg

BEAR CLAWS

BEAR CLAWS

1. Make one recipe of
Basic Pastry Dough (p. 124)

2. Keep board well
floured and roll out in
approximately a 6 x 18
inch rectangle.

3. Apply Date Spread
thinly on half of the long
side of the rectangle. (p. 105).

4. Fold the rectangle—
the long way—over and
press edges together.
Cut in five inch sections
and then cut one inch
slits from folded side
about half way through.
If desired, sprinkle top
with toasted coconut and
ground walnuts .

DATE SPREAD

DATE SPREAD

2½ cups date pieces

1 cup water

1 tsp. lemon juice

1 tsp. vanilla

1 tsp. grated orange rind

¼ tsp. salt

Bring all ingredients to a
boil on stove or in microwave, and simmer to
make a thick paste. Or,
blend in blender using
hot water, adding a little
extra if needed to blend
thick and smooth.

Prep. time: 10 min.

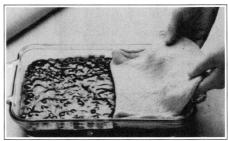

DESSERTS

A ll around the world, human beings have cultivated a craving for rich, sweet endings to their meals. We call it dessert—that pleasurable experience that both entices children into eating their greens and rewards us for surviving our hard day at work. Dessert has worked its way into every

From the left: Raisin-Bran Muffins and Kimberley's Trifle Cake

phase of our life. No memory from being at grandma's house to our birthday parties would be right without dessert. But this irresistibly delicious friend has turned enemy more times than we want to remember. The cavities in our mouth and the spare tire around our middle, to a great degree, owe their existence to dessert!

127

Desserts—Sweeteners

If there is any hope of actually getting the upper hand in the battle against your sweet tooth, we believe it is by providing yourself and your family with an alternative. We do not believe healthy means, "If it tastes good, spit it out!" So, for years we have experimented with untold combinations of unrefined sugars, fats, grains and carbohydrates to replace the deadly desserts we had come to love. A few outstanding and timeless masterpieces have emerged which tantalize even the most discriminating palate. When you learn to make these delicious replacements, you will be delighted to discover that giving up those calorie-packed sweets is easy.

"Because it is the fashion, in harmony with morbid appetite, rich cake, pies, and puddings, and every hurtful thing, are crowded into the stomach. The table must be loaded down with a variety, or the depraved appetite cannot be satisfied. In the morning, these slaves to appetite often have impure breath, and a furred tongue. They do not enjoy health, and wonder why they suffer with pains, headaches, and various ills."
Counsels on Diet and Foods, p. 332

Much has happened in the last 15 or 20 years to change the selections available on the shelves of our supermarkets. We see such things as "fat free," or "fruit juice sweetened." We have several options now, other than refined sugar, for sweetening our desserts. Here are a few from which you can choose according to your taste and their availability.

Desserts—Sweeteners

Honey: Honey contains some minerals and vitamins not found in sugar, and because it is a bit sweeter, less honey can be used than sugar.

Sucanat: Cane juice, dehydrated and crystallized; this is a very unrefined form of sugar. It is found in health food stores, and is brown, dry, and granulated in appearance, so keep in mind that it will give the recipe a darker color. It is a very tasty sweetener for cookies, but is about half as sweet as sugar.

Fructose: Sugar refined from fruit instead of beets or cane. It makes little difference from table sugar to our bodies, but is slightly sweeter, so less can be used.

Dates: Nutritionally, dates are superior to honey, but for most purposes need to be blended in with the liquid ingredients, or used as date sugar.

Fruit juice sweeteners/concentrates: The most readily available is apple juice concentrate, found in the frozen food section of any supermarket. A recent newcomer to the natural food stores is a fruit juice syrup that is about twice as concentrated as apple juice concentrate. It is usually a combination of peach, pear, and pineapple and the most common brand is "Mystic Lake Fruit Sweetener." Tree Top makes one that is available in bakery supply wholesale outlets, and some natural food stores and co-ops carry it in bulk. We call this product "fruit sweetener" in the recipes; the combination of these three has a milder flavor than concentrated apple juice and is preferred in most recipes because it gives less of an acidic or fruity taste.

Date Sweetener: This is a combination of three sweeteners: dates, honey, and apple juice. By combining the three, the characteristic flavor of honey, dates, or fruit juice is masked and the result is a pleasant sweetness similar to brown sugar.

DATE SWEETENER

PRUNE SAUCE

DATE SWEETENER

2 cups date pieces

2 cups honey

2 cups conc. apple juice

Place all in blender and blend smooth. Store unused portion in refrigerator. It will keep for weeks. If your date pieces are hard, you may need to soften them by bringing them to a boil in a small amount of water before blending.

PRUNE SAUCE

Prune Sauce is very useful in cakes, muffins, and cookies to replace fat. It has a quality when blended that is slippery and moist, and in baking it gives the same rich, moist effect without the grease. Be sure to try our Carob-Prune Cake.

Directions

Blend 2½ cups soft pitted prunes with 8 cups water until very smooth. This can be done in the blender, but also works great in a food processor. If prunes are hard, bring to a boil, turn off heat and let stand to soften about 30 minutes before blending. Make a double recipe and keep in the refrigerator or freezer for future use.

Desserts—Cakes

Making a fat-free cake is a challenge for the most experienced of cooks. Add to that a sugar-free, egg-free, baking-powderless cake, and what do you have left? That's what we thought, and for a time we didn't attempt cakes. We'll stick to pies and cobblers, we decided. But we had so many requests, we began experimenting. What we have come up with would never win the Pillsbury Bake-off prize, but is sold daily at Five Loaves to many satisfied, health-conscious customers. The secret in making a fat-free cake moist is applesauce. We also use it in our muffins and breads with great success. *See p. 136 for more tips.*

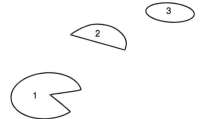

Photo key:

1. **Carrot Cake with Creamy Cashew Glaze**
2. **Carob Cake with Coconut Pecan Topping**
3. **Cashew Cheese Cake**

131

Desserts—Cakes

APPLE OR BLUEBERRY CRUMBCAKE

CRUMB TOPPING

APPLE CRUMBCAKE

3 cups flour (may use whole wheat pastry and unbleached white, or barley or oat flour)

3 Tbs. Ener-G Baking Powder (or 1½ tsp. Rumford)

1 tsp. salt

1 cup water

⅔ cup applesauce

½ cup conc. fruit sweetener, date sweetener, or honey

2 tsp. vanilla

3 cups Apple Filling (p. 10) or Blueberry Sauce (p. 7)

1. Stir together in a small bowl the water, applesauce, fruit sweetener, and vanilla.

2. Stir in the flours, baking powder and salt; beat briskly with a spoon until well mixed.

3. Spread half of cake batter in the bottom of a 9 x 13 inch pan that has been sprayed with Pam.

4. Spoon and carefully spread fruit filling over the cake batter, and if desired, sprinkle Apple Filling with raisins.

5. Spread remaining batter over the top and sprinkle chopped walnuts, coconut, or Crumb Topping on top.

6. Bake at 350° for about 30 to 40 minutes or until golden brown.

Prep. time: 20 min.
Baking time: 30 - 40 min.

CRUMB TOPPING

1 cup quick oats

¼ cup each date sugar and fructose or ¾ cup Sucanat

¼ cup chopped walnuts

¼ cup Tahini or almond butter

¼ cup molasses

½ tsp. salt

3 Tbs. applesauce

1. Mix together all but the applesauce.

2. Stir in the applesauce, adding more or less as needed to gain a soft, but not too wet mix that can be crumbled on top of crumbcake, cobbler, muffins, or fruit crisp before baking.

Prep. time: 8 min.

Makes 12 servings

Nutrient Information
Per Serving

CALORIES	212
PROTEIN	7%
FAT	2% / .6 gm
CARBOHYDRATE	91%
SODIUM	196 mg

Makes 2 cups

Nutrient Information
Serving

CALORIES	299
PROTEIN	7%
FAT	3% / .9 gm
CARBOHYDRATE	90%
SODIUM	mg

CAROB-PRUNE CAKE

Here is our version of that old favorite—chocolate prune cake. Carob comes in two shades—the darker one is made from toasted carob and will give your food a richer, deeper color.

Why do we use carob instead of chocolate? Chocolate contains two chemical stimulants: caffeine and theobromine and some prefer not to use it (see table and discussion, p. 167). Carob isn't bitter and doesn't require as much sweetening. But you won't feel as if you are missing anything once you try this simple-to-make cake. Notice that it is fat free. The prunes have a special quality that take the place of fat when blended, giving this cake its characteristic moistness and texture.

1 cup date pieces

1 cup honey

¾ cups hot water

½ cup soft pitted prunes (about 10 prunes)

½ cup applesauce

1 Tbs. vanilla

½ cup carob powder

1 tsp. Pero, Roma, or other instant coffee substitute

1 tsp. Kitchen Bouquet (omit if you are using the darker, toasted carob powder)

2¼ cups flour (best to use 1 cup white pastry or cake flour and 1¼ cups whole wheat pastry flour)

2 Tbs. Ener-G baking powder or 1 Tbs. regular baking powder

¾ tsp. salt

½ cup water

1. **Preheat oven and prepare cake pans.**

Hint: It is important to place this in the oven soon after mixing when using Ener-G baking powder for leavening since it begins to act as soon as mixed with a liquid.

2. **Blend together the dates, honey, hot water and prunes and add vanilla, carob powder, coffee substitute and Kitchen Bouquet if you use it.**

3. **In a separate mixing bowl, stir together the flours and salt. Add the blended mixture (and remaining half cup water if needed) and beat with electric mixer about one minute, or longer if by hand. Batter should be soft but stiff enough to hold its shape.**

4. **Have pans ready and oven pre-heated.**

5. **Stir baking powder into the mix and pour immediately into 2 - 8 inch cake pans or a sheet pan* and bake for 25-35 minutes at 350°.**

5. **Cool on racks, and frost with Carob Frosting (next page).**

*This cake will not cook in the center if the batter is too deep. Any pan can be used but fill to only 1 inch depth. An 8 inch Bundt pan which holds no more than 1½ qts. will work because of the increased baking surface. If the middle is gummy, bake longer, but this risks over-cooking or burning the edges. So use a shallow batter!

Hint: For a layer cake, use Coconut-Pecan Filling (p. 134) between layers. If using decorative flan pans that leave a depression in the top of the cake, frost the edge with Carob Frosting (p. 134) and then fill the depression with Coconut Pecan Filling or, with chilled, re-blended Carob Pudding (p. 157). In this case, chill for 1 hour before serving so it will set up.

Prep. time: 30 min.
Baking time: 30 min.

Makes 15 servings

Nutrient Information
Per Serving

CALORIES	431
PROTEIN	6%
FAT	4% / 2 gm
CARBOHYDRATE	90%

CAROB FROSTING

COCONUT PECAN

CAROB FROSTING

2 cups dates

⅓ cup carob powder

½ cup honey or conc. fruit sweetener

1 cup water

1 tsp. vanilla

1 tsp. Pero or Roma (coffee substitute)

2 Tbs. peanut butter

2 pitted prunes

½ tsp. salt

1. Blend all together in the blender until very smooth.

Hint: This is a very thick mix and you will have to help it through the blades by carefully scraping the sides of the blender while blending. A little extra water may need to be added to help it blend smooth, depending on how dry your dates are. If your dates are very dry, they will need to be softened before blending by bringing them to a boil with a small amount of water and letting them stand for 20 minutes. Blend for at least two minutes until very smooth. If you want thicker frosting, you can add 1 to 2 tablespoons of Instant Clear Jel and blend for one minute longer.

2. Spread on the cooled cake and sprinkle with chopped walnuts or coconut, if desired.

Prep. time: 12 minutes

COCONUT-PECAN FILLING

1½ Tbs. cornstarch

½ cup water

½ cup honey or conc. fruit sweetener

½ tsp. coconut extract

1 tsp. maple flavoring

½ cup coconut

½ cup coarsely chopped walnuts or pecans*

1. Place cornstarch in a small sauce pan and gradually stir in the ½ cup water; add remaining ingredients.

2. Bring to a boil, and remove from heat. Let cool about 30 minutes before using on cake.

*For a better flavor, toast walnuts or pecans in oven at 375° for 10 min., watching carefully that you don't burn them.

*Prep. time: 10 min.
Cooking time: 5 min.*

Makes 2 cups

Nutrient Information
Per Serving

CALORIES	108
PROTEIN	4%
FAT	9% / gm
CARBOHYDRATE	87%
SODIUM	77 mg

Makes 1¼ cups

Nutrient Information
Per Serving (2 Tbs.)

CALORIES	132
PROTEIN	3%
FAT	47% / 7.4 gm
CARBOHYDRATE	50%
SODIUM	4 mg

CARROT CAKE

CREAMY CASHEW GLAZE

CARROT CAKE

2 cups Date Sweetener (p. 130)

2 Tbs. orange juice conc.

1 tsp. vanilla

1 cup applesauce or prune sauce

½ cup water

½ tsp. cardamom

½ tsp. coriander

2 cups grated carrots

¾ cup walnuts

¾ cup shredded coconut

3 Tbs. fructose (opt.)

1 cup raisins

1½ cups unbleached white flour

1½ cups whole wheat pastry flour

3 Tbs. Ener-G baking powder or 1½ Tbs. regular baking powder

1¼ tsp. salt

1. Prepare a 11 x 17 inch sheet pan or two 9-inch round cake pans and have them ready for the batter as soon as it is mixed.

2. In a large mixing bowl, stir together all the ingredients except the flours, baking powder, salt and raisins.

3. Sift together flours into a separate bowl along with baking powder and salt. Mix in the raisins to coat them with flour and keep them from clumping.

4. Stir dry mix into the wet mix and beat with a spoon for about ½ minute, adding a bit more water if it seems too stiff. Batter should be soft, but stiff enough to spread and hold its shape.

5. Spoon into the prepared pans immediately and place in 350° oven for about 30 minutes *(see Carob Cake baking tips on p. 133)*. Test with toothpick (insert and remove—see if clean). Cool and ice with Creamy Cashew Glaze (p. 135) or Whipped Topping (p. 156)

Prep. time: 45 min.
Baking time: 30 min.

CREAMY CASHEW GLAZE

1 cup cashews

1 cup water

⅔ cup fructose

¼ tsp. salt

4 tsp. powdered vanilla, or 2 Tbs. liquid vanilla

½ cup **Better Than Milk Lite** powder (or other soy milk powder)

3 - 5 Tbs. (or more) Instant Clear Jel

1. Blend the first 5 ingredients together until very smooth.

2. While blender is still on, add the milk powder and Clear Jel. If not thick enough, add more Clear Jel until spreading consistency. It is easier to do this step in the food processor because it can better handle a thick mix.

Prep. time: 10 min.

Makes 16 servings

Nutrient Information
Per Serving
CALORIES	355
PROTEIN	6%
FAT	30% / 13 gm
CARBOHYDRATE	64%
SODIUM	149 mg

Makes 2 cups

Nutrient Information
Per Serving (2 Tbs.)
CALORIES	47
PROTEIN	7%
FAT	39% / 2 gm
CARBOHYDRATE	54%
SODIUM	18 mg

SPICE CAKE

2 cups prune sauce or applesauce

2½ cups Date Sweetener (p. 130)

1 Tbs. molasses

1 Tbs. vanilla

1½ cups whole wheat pastry flour

2 cups unbleached white flour

3 ½ Tbs. Ener-G Baking Powder

1¼ tsp. salt

1 tsp. cardamom

1 tsp. coriander

⅛ tsp. anise

1 cup walnuts

1½ cup raisins

1. Mix together in a large bowl the prune sauce, date sweetener, molasses, and vanilla.

2. Stir in the remaining ingredients, mixing well.

3. Spread into two 9 inch round cake pans or a 11 x 17 inch sheet pan.

4. Bake for about 30 minutes at 350°.

Prep. time: 30 min.
Baking time: 30 min.

Cake Baking Tip:

We like to bake our vegan cakes in shallow sheet pans—spreading batter no thicker than 1 inch. This eliminates problems with gummy centers and dried out edges (when eggs are not used).

Shallow cakes are excellent for layering or for making tortes.

Makes 12 - 16 servings

Nutrient Information
Per Serving

CALORIES	327
PROTEIN	7%
FAT	12% / 5.5 gm
CARBOHYDRATE	81%
SODIUM	176 mg

Desserts—Pies

Here are some of our best customer-tested pie recipes. The pumpkin pie is served at Five Loaves almost daily, and people love it even though it's low in fat and uses less spicy seasonings.

Coconut Cream Pie, Apple Crisp with Whipped Topping and Pumpkin Pie

Desserts—Pies

PIE CRUST

PIE CRUST

1 cup barley flour (or ½ cup quick oatmeal and ½ cup whole wheat pastry or white flour)

1 tsp. salt

⅓ cup nut butter or ⅔ cup fine nut meal

⅓ cup or more water

Hint: Nut butter can be made in a food processor using cashews, Brazil nuts, almonds, or just about any nut, keeping in mind that darker nuts will make a darker crust. A fine nut meal can be made in your food processor or blender and is simply the product of less blending.

1. Mix nut butter into dry ingredients with hands until well distributed throughout.

2. Add water and gently knead dough into a ball, adding a bit more water if needed for a soft, but not sticky, ball of dough.

3. Roll the dough from center to edges, forming a 12-inch circle.

Makes one 9″ shell

Nutrient Information
Per Serving (1/6 crust)
CALORIES	116
PROTEIN	9%
FAT	37% / 4.9 gm
CARBOHYDRATE	54%
SODIUM	268 mg

CRUMBLE PIE CRUST

Hint: This is most easily done by rolling between two pieces of plastic bag material. Remove the top piece of plastic and invert the pie plate over the rolled-out dough. Slip hand under the bottom plastic with pie dough and plate on top. Quickly flip it over so the dough is now over the plate, and peel off the plastic. Gently shape the dough into the plate with fingers, patching where necessary. This dough is very workable and patches well.

4. Trim pastry to ½ inch beyond edge of plate. Fold under extra pastry and crimp edge.

5. For a pre-baked crust, prick bottom and sides of pastry generously with the tines of a fork. Prick where bottom and sides meet all around the pie shell. Bake in a 400° oven for 10 to 12 minutes or until golden.

6. For a double crust pie, make 1½ times the recipe and fill unbaked pastry with your choice of fruit filling. Slit top in several places and bake until done.

Prep. time: 30 min.
Baking time: 10 min.
(either crusts)

CRUMBLE PIE CRUST

Approx. 1 cup Granola (p. 17) or ¾ cup Grape Nuts cereal

¾ cup unsweetened, flaked coconut or nuts such as walnuts

⅓ cup Sucanat or date sugar (dates that are not too moist may be used)

Approx. 2 Tbs. water

1. Place all ingredients except water in a blender, and make into fine crumbs.

2. Pour crumbs into a small mixing bowl and stir in the water. Mix together until all is moistened, adding more water if needed to make the mix just moist enough to stick together when pressed against the side of the bowl, but not too wet and sticky.

3. Press into a Pam-sprayed pie plate, shaping with fingers to make a nicely formed pie crust.

4. Bake at 375° for about 10 minutes.

Makes one 9″ shell

Nutrient Information
Per Serving (1/6 crust)
CALORIES	104
PROTEIN	6%
FAT	17% / 2 gm
CARBOHYDRATE	77%
SODIUM	82 mg

Desserts—Pies

COCONUT-OAT PIE CRUST

ORCHARD APPLE PIE

COCONUT-OAT PIE CRUST

1½ cups rolled oats (either quick or old fashioned)

1½ cups unsweetened flaked coconut

½ cup Sucanat

1 tsp. salt

¼ cup water

1. Place all ingredients except water in a food processor and blend into fine crumbs (can also be done in blender).

2. Add water and blend briefly to mix. (If using a blender, pour into a bowl before mixing in the water by hand.)

3. May be rolled our or finger-pressed into two pie plates.

4. Bake at 375° for 10 minutes.

Makes 2 - 9" pie shells

Nutrient Information
Per Serving (1/6 crust)

CALORIES	131
PROTEIN	7%
FAT	53% / 8.1 gm
CARBOHYDRATE	40%
SODIUM	182 mg

OLD FASHIONED ORCHARD APPLE PIE

7-8 cups thinly sliced cooking apples

⅓ cup unbleached white flour or ¼ cup cornstarch

½ cup Sucanat or Evaporated cane juice (or ⅓ cup sugar)

1 rounded tsp. coriander

½ tsp. salt

¼ cup apple juice concentrate

1 tsp. vanilla

1 tsp. coconut flavoring (opt.)

1. Mix together the dry ingredients and stir into sliced apples coating them evenly. Mound apples in unbaked bottom crust (see below), and cover with top crust. Trim and flute edges and prick top crust with a fork.

2. Use aluminum foil strips to wrap-cover crust edges. Bake on a cookie sheet to catch drips (a wide mouth mason jar ring under the pie also keeps the pie plate clean).

Hint: Want a great pie? Bake well (even 1½ hrs. - apples should not feel crispy when pierced with sharp knife) at 350°.

DOUBLE CRUST

¾ cup whole wheat pastry or unbleached white flour

¾ cup quick oatmeal

1 cup Brazil nut meal*

1 tsp. salt

½ cup water

*Make Brazil nut meal by placing Brazil nuts in a food processor and blending into a fine meal, but not to the stage of becoming oily or buttery. Almonds or walnuts may be used, but Brazil's are best.

1. Place all ingredients except water in a mixing bowl and mix together with hands until evenly mixed.

2. Add the ½ cup water and mix with hands, forming a dough ball that holds together. If it seems dry and some of the oats and flour aren't sticking to the ball, add a bit more water, but not so much that it becomes wet and sticky.

3. Divide into 2 balls of dough, one slightly larger than the other. Using the larger ball, roll between 2 sheets of plastic and line pie plate. Fill with fruit and top with remaining crust.

139

PUMPKIN PIE

PUMPKIN CHIFFON PIE

OLD FASHIONED BAKED PUMPKIN PIE

1¾ cups cooked pumpkin (15 oz. can)

1 - 15 oz. can coconut milk

*Tip: The pie is wonderful with coconut milk but two lower fat options are:
1. Use ½ can coconut milk with ½ can of water or
2. Two cups soy milk or nut milk.*

½ cup pitted dates

½ cup honey

1/4 cup cornstarch

1 tsp. vanilla

½ tsp. coriander

½ tsp. salt

1. Blend all ingredients in the blender until smooth.

2. Pour into an unbaked pie shell and bake for 1 hr.

Makes 1 - 9" pie

Nutrient Information
Per Serving (1/6 shell)

CALORIES	284
PROTEIN	7%
FAT	28% / 9.8 gm
CARBOHYDRATE	65%
SODIUM	407 mg

PUMPKIN PIE (no-bake)

1½ cups hot water

½ cup cashew nuts

½ cup pitted dates

¾ stick agar or 1 rounded Tbs. flake agar or 2 Tbs. Emes Kosher Jel

½ cup honey or conc. fruit sweetener

1 tsp. vanilla

½ tsp. maple flavoring

½ tsp. coriander

½ tsp. salt

1¾ cups cooked pumpkin or yams

1. Boil water and Emes Kosher Jel or Agar for one full minute.

2. Place hot water and agar mixture in blender and add all the remaining ingredients except the pumpkin. Start blender on low, then advance to high. Blend for at least one minute until smooth.

3. Stir blended mix into cooked pumpkin - mix well in a mixing bowl.

4. Pour blended pumpkin into a 9-inch pre-baked pie crust.

5. Chill until set.

Prep. time: 20 min.

PUMPKIN CHIFFON PIE

1. Make Pumpkin Pie filling using Emes Kosher Jel variation

Hint: Agar won't work—after re-blending, it won't set up again!

2. Chill two hours before filling crust as follows:

3. Place chilled pumpkin filling in blender and add 1½ cups chilled Whipped Topping (p. 156). Blend together briefly.

4. Mound into pre-baked pie crust. Chill and serve.

Variation: In step # 2 for Pumpkin Pie, add ⅛ orange peel and ⅛ tsp. lemon extract.

Makes 1 - 9" pie

Nutrient Information
Per Serving (1/6 pie)

CALORIES	279
PROTEIN	5%
FAT	18% / 6 gm
CARBOHYDRATE	77%
SODIUM	203 mg

Desserts—Pies

LEMON CHIFFON*

KEY LIME PIE

LEMON CHIFFON

2 cups pineapple juice

2 Tbs. Emes Kosher Jel (unflavored)

¼ cup honey

1 cup water

2 Tbs. fresh lemon juice

¼ tsp. grated lemon rind

¼ cup orange juice conc.

2 cups Whipped Topping (p. 156)

1. Bring water to a boil and add Emes gelatin; stir until dissolved. Stir in remaining ingredients. Place in refrigerator to set up.

2. When firm, place in blender with 2 cups Whipped Topping (p. 156) and blend until smooth.

3. Pour into baked pie crust and chill until firm. Garnish with lemon twist and mint, or top with Whipped Topping if desired.

Prep. time: 30 min.

Makes one 9″ pie

Nutrient Information
Per Serving (1/8 pie)
CALORIES	223
PROTEIN	8%
FAT	31% / 8.1 gm
CARBOHYDRATE	61%
SODIUM	61 mg

LEMON CREAM

(simple Lemon Chiffon variation)

2 cups pineapple juice

2 Tbs. lemon juice

1 tsp. grated lemon rind

¼ cup honey

¾ cup coconut milk (½ can)

5 Tbs. cornstarch

1. Blend all ingredients together. You can use a blender, but whisking it together in a bowl is satisfactory as long as the cornstarch is completely dissolved and there are no lumps.

2. Cook in a heavy sauce pan on the top of the stove, stirring constantly, until mixture becomes thick and boils slightly.

3. Poor immediately into prepared pie crust. Place in refrigerator to cool.

4. Slice and serve when pie has thoroughly cooled. Garnish with a slice of lemon or top with Whipped Topping (p. 156).

KEY LIME PIE

1 - 12 oz. can frozen white grape juice conc.

4 Tbs. Emes Kosher Jel

1 - 10½ oz. can coconut milk

1 brick firm tofu (14 oz.)

⅔ cup brown rice syrup

Juice and grated peel of 2 limes

1 Tbs. vanilla

½ tsp. salt

6 drops green food coloring

1. Mix together the Emes Kosher Gel and white grape juice concentrate in a small saucepan; bring to a boil.

2. Place in blender along with coconut milk and tofu; blend until smooth.

3. Combine blended mixture with remaining ingredients in a mixing bowl, beating with a spoon or wire whip until well mixed.

4. Pour into 2 pre-baked pie shells and chill until set.

Makes 2 - 9″ pies

Nutrient Information
Per Serving (1/6 pie)
CALORIES	204
PROTEIN	12%
FAT	20% / 10 gm
CARBOHYDRATE	68%
SODIUM	180 mg

COCONUT CREAM

NO-MEAT MINCE

COCONUT CREAM

1½ cups water

½ cup unsweetened, shredded coconut

1 cup soy (or coconut) milk

½ cup cashew nuts

¾ cup honey

1½ tsp. salt

¾ cup cold water

1 cup tofu

3 Tbs. Emes Kosher Jel

1 tsp. vanilla

2 tsp. coconut flavoring

1½ cups coconut*

1. Place 1½ cups water and ½ cup coconut in a saucepan and simmer 10 minutes. Then stir in Emes Kosher Jel.

2. Place hot coconut mixture in blender along with soy milk, cashew nuts, honey, and salt. Blend for about 2 minutes.

Coconut in two places in recipe

3. Turn off blender and add remaining ingredients except the last 1½ cups coconut. Blend a few seconds and then pour into a bowl. Fold in the coconut and place in refrigerator to chill until set up.

Hint: Chilling process can be speeded up by placing in a shallow metal pan.

4. Whip up by stirring with a spoon or wire whip and spoon into 2 pre-baked pie shells. Chill about an hour to set up again.

Prep. time: 30 min.
Cooking time: 10 min.

NO-MEAT MINCE

2 cups finely diced apples

½ cup pitted prunes, diced small

1 cup raisins

½ cup honey

¼ cup frozen orange juice conc.

Juice from 1 lemon plus some of the rind

3 Tbs. flour

1. Make a double-crust pie recipe and place rolled-out crust in pie plate.

2. Mix together all the ingredients and place in the uncooked bottom crust.

3. Roll out top crust and put in place, fluting edges and slitting the top for the steam to escape.

4. Bake at 350° for 45 to 50 minutes.

Prep. time: 40 min.
Baking time: 45 min.

Makes 2 - 9" pies

Nutrient Information
Per Serving (1 piece)

CALORIES	262
PROTEIN	8%
FAT	44% / 13.6 gm
CARBOHYDRATE	48%
SODIUM	474 mg

Makes 1 - 9" pie

Nutrient Information
Per Serving (1/6 pie)

CALORIES	302
PROTEIN	6%
FAT	14% / 5.2 gm
CARBOHYDRATE	80%
SODIUM	272 mg

Desserts—Pies

APPLE CRISP

APPLE TURNOVERS

APPLE CRISP

1 recipe of Apple Filling (p. 10)

CRISP TOPPING*

½ cup fine almond meal or Brazil nut butter

½ cup barley flour or whole wheat flour

½ tsp. salt

1 cup quick oats

¼ cup unsweetened coconut

¼ cup hot water

¼ cup honey

1. Mix dry ingredients in a bowl.

2. Dissolve honey in the hot water and add to the dry ingredients.

> *Hint: Mix together until all the moisture is evenly distributed. It will be soft and somewhat sticky like oatmeal cookies, but not dry and powdery.*

3. Place apple filling in a 9 x 13 inch baking dish. Use fingers to distribute crisp topping evenly over the hot apples.

> *Hint: This will take a little time and patience because the sticky mixture will need to be crumbled and placed methodically over the whole area. It doesn't just slip into place like an oily mixture would. But it is worth the effort, because when baked it looks and tastes very good.*

4. Bake in a 350° oven for 15 - 20 minutes until golden brown on top.

> *Prep. time: 30 min.*
> *Cooking time: 20 min.*

> **Apple Crisp is made, as you can see, by putting the "topping" over Apple Filling. Try the same topping with any of the fruit toppings on pp. 6 - 11.*

APPLE TURNOVERS

Make a double recipe of Pie Crust (p. 138) and one recipe of Apple Filling (p. 10).

1. Divide pie pastry into 8 balls and roll into circles between 2 sheets of plastic.

2. Place on a cookie sheet and spoon about ⅓ cup of filling on one side of the center and fold over the other half to form a turnover; crimp or flute the edges.

> *Hint: Use any of the fruit fillings in the Breakfast section for turnovers using regular Clear Jel for the thickening agent instead of cornstarch. If you make your fillings with enough Clear Jel to be thick and not runny, you will not have the problem of the sauce boiling out of the crust as it bakes.*

3. Bake at 350° for about 20 minutes or until golden brown.

> *Prep. time: 45 min.*
> *Baking time: 20 min.*

Makes 9 x 13 inch dessert

Nutrient Information
Per Serving (1/12 piece)

CALORIES	109
PROTEIN	10%
FAT	43% / 5.5 gm
CARBOHYDRATE	47%
SODIUM	74 mg

Makes 8 turnovers

Nutrient Information
Per Serving (1 turnover)

CALORIES	48
PROTEIN	8%
FAT	26% /1.5 gm
CARBOHYDRATE	66%
SODIUM	69 mg

Desserts—Cookies

Few things will bring a smile as fast as a plate full of homemade cookies. Store-bought cookies simply don't compare, in taste or ingredients. We have tried using Calcium Carbonate (Ener-G Baking Powder) in cookies but with poor results. The sour taste seems quite noticeable here where it isn't in cakes or muffins. We are using Featherlite Baking Powder or none at all in our cookies.

From the left: Crunchy Clusters,* Oatmeal Raisin Cookies, Almond Jewels and Carob-Peanut Butter Pinwheels

*Crunchy Clusters can be shipped to you from Five Loaves! Order by phone (206 726-7989) or mail with credit card or personal check. Popcorn Balls in this section are a nice option!

Desserts—Cookies

OATMEAL-RAISIN

BANANA-DATE

OATMEAL-RAISIN

1½ cups barley flour or whole wheat pastry flour

1½ Tbs. Featherlite or Rumford baking powder (may omit, but cookies will have a different texture)

1¼ tsp. salt

¼ tsp. each cardamom and coriander (opt.)

1 cup nut butter (refer to appendix for details. Brazil nut butter is very good in this)

4 cups quick oats

3 cups raisins

2 cups Date Sweetener (p. 130) or use 1½ cups Sucanat and 1 cup water.

2 cups applesauce*

2 tsp. vanilla

1. Mix together first 4 ingredients into a large mixing bowl.

2. Add the nut butter and mix together with hands until well distributed throughout.

3. Stir in oats and raisins and then remaining ingredients. Mix well.

4. Place on cookie sheet with a ¼ cup ice cream scoop and flatten slightly with a rubber spatula dipped in water, or leave in mounds.

5. Bake for 20 minutes at 350°, or until lightly browned on the top and bottom.

Hint: For best baking results, bake toward the top of the oven or on a double cookie sheet to prevent the bottom from burning before the top browns.

Prep. time: 15 min.
Baking time: 20 min.

*Or 2 cups flaxseed gel (boil 2 Tbs. flaxseed in 2 cups water for five minutes— strain out seeds)

BANANA DATE

3 large ripe bananas

½ tsp. salt

1 Tbs. vanilla

2 cups quick oats

1 cup chopped dates

1 cup raisins or currants

½ cup dried papaya and pineapple chunks

½ cup chopped walnuts (opt.)

1. Peel and mash bananas in a mixing bowl with a potato masher. Add remaining ingredients and mix well.

2. Drop onto a cookie sheet with two spoons or a small scoop. Keep mounded up rather than flattened.

3. Bake at 350° for 20 to 30 minutes.

Prep. time: 15 min.
Baking time: 20 - 30 min.

Makes 24 cookies

Nutrient Information
Per Serving
CALORIES   225
PROTEIN   7%
FAT   22% / 5.9 gm
CARBOHYDRATE   71%
SODIUM   149 mg

Makes 35 small cookies

Nutrient Information
Per Serving
CALORIES   70
PROTEIN   7%
FAT   15% / 1.5 gm
CARBOHYDRATE   78%
SODIUM   32 mg

Desserts—Cookies

PINEAPPLE DATE BARS

APRICOT PINEAPPLE BARS

PINEAPPLE-DATE

1½ cups barley flour (wheat or white okay)

½ cup Brazil nut butter

¾ tsp. salt

2 cups quick oats

½ cup unsweetened, flaked coconut

½ cup water and ½ cup honey, mixed together

1 cup pineapple chunks and juice or crushed pineapple

1 cup date pieces

1 tsp. vanilla

1 cup raisins

1 cup diced dried pineapple

1. Place flour and salt in a mixing bowl and add the Brazil nut butter. Work evenly together with your hands, then stir in salt, oats, and co-conut. Then add honey and water mixture to the dry mix and stir together.

Hint: The mix should be moist with all the dry mix evenly coated, but not too wet and gummy.

4. Place half the mixture on the bottom of a 9 x 13 inch pan that has been oiled or sprayed; press with fingers like pie crust. Bake 10 minutes at 350°.

5. Meanwhile, blend dates and canned pineapple. Spread over baked crust.

6. Sprinkle evenly with raisins and dried pineapple.

7. Sprinkle remaining crust mixture evenly over the top. Press gently into pineapple-date filling with fingers.

8. Bake 20 - 30 minutes at 350° until lightly browned. Remove and cool before cutting in squares.

Note: A single recipe fits a 9 x 13 inch pan. If you are making cookies for a crowd, a double recipe fits on a cookie sheet and makes 24-30 bars.

APRICOT-PINEAPPLE

Double recipe of the topping in Apple Crisp (p. 143)

Half recipe of Apricot Sauce (p. 7) (about 3 cups)

1 cup diced dried pineapple

½ cup shredded coconut (opt.)

1. Press half of the Crisp Topping into a 9 x 13 inch non-stick pan or Pam sprayed baking dish. Place in pre-heated oven and bake for 10 minutes at 375°.

2. Remove from oven. Stir diced dried pineapple into Apricot Sauce and spread over the baked bottom crust.

3. Distribute remaining crisp topping evenly over the top with fingers, and sprinkle with shredded coconut if desired. Bake in 350° oven for 15 - 20

Makes 12 - 15 bars

Nutrient Information
Per Serving

CALORIES	283
PROTEIN	7%
FAT	16% / 5.7 gm
CARBOHYDRATE	77%
SODIUM	111 mg

Makes 12 - 15 bars

Nutrient Information
Per Serving

CALORIES	147
PROTEIN	7%
FAT	40% / 7.1 gm
CARBOHYDRATE	53%
SODIUM	75 mg

Desserts—Cookies

PEANUT BUTTER

OATMEAL LEMON

PERSIMMON

PEANUT BUTTER

1½ cups dry roasted peanuts

1¼ cup whole wheat pastry flour

½ tsp. salt (unsalted peanuts)

½ cup honey

2 Tbs. water*

1 Tbs. vanilla

1. Place peanuts, flour, and salt in food processor. Blend together until nuts are as fine as the flour; takes about 1 minute.

Hint: Blending the flour with the nuts keeps the nuts from caking and makes it easy to mix. Over-blending will cause the nuts to become oily and should be avoided.

2. Meanwhile, heat the honey slightly. Remove nut and flour mixture to a bowl and stir in the honey, vanilla and water. Mix until it becomes a dough like pie crust. A bit more water may be added if the mixture seems too dry, but be careful not to get the dough wet or sticky. It should be dry enough to handle and still stick together in a ball.

3. Form balls the size of walnuts and place on a cookie sheet. Press each ball flat with the palm of your hand and then with a fork to about ¼ inch thick.

*Bake at 350° for 10 minutes until just beginning to turn golden brown. It is better to under-bake than to over-bake (burn!) peanut butter cookies. *Without a food processor: use 1 cup peanut butter and omit extra water.*

OATMEAL LEMON

1 cup cashew nuts

2 cups flaxseed gel
(boil 2 Tbs. flaxseed in 2 cups water for five minutes—strain out seeds)

1 tsp. salt

1 tsp. maple

1 tsp. vanilla

½ tsp. lemon extract

2 cups Sucanat or 1½ cups Brown sugar

3 cups each quick and regular oatmeal

2 cups raisins

1 cup unsweetened shredded coconut, opt.

1 Tbs. Ener-G baking powder

1. Blend cashews, flax gel and seasonings.

2. Mix dry ingredients together; then stir into blended mixture.

3. Place on cookie sheet; bake at 400° for 20 minutes until lightly browned.

PERSIMMON

1 cup whole wheat pastry flour

1 Tbs. Featherlight Baking Powder (or substitute)

1 tsp. salt

¾ cup Brazil nut meal or butter

2 cups quick oats

1½ cups raisins

1 cup chopped walnuts

1 cup persimmon pulp

1¼ cups Date Sweetener (p. 130) (or 2 cups persimmon pulp and ¼ cup honey)

½ tsp. cardamom

1. Combine first 5 ingredients in a mixing bowl.

2. Stir in oats, raisins, and walnuts; then Date Sweetener. Mix well.

3. Spoon or scoop onto a cookie sheet and bake at 350° for 15 or 20 minutes. (see Oatmeal Raisin Cookies baking tip, p. 145)

Prep. time: 15 min.
Baking time: 15 - 20 min.

Makes 15 cookies

Nutrient Information
Per Serving

CALORIES	166
PROTEIN	11%
FAT	44% / 9 gm
CARBOHYDRATE	45%
SODIUM	123 mg

Makes 30 cookies

Nutrient Information
Per Serving

CALORIES	188
PROTEIN	8%
FAT	19% / 4 gm
CARBOHYDRATE	73%
SODIUM	82 mg

Makes 24 cookies

Nutrient Information
Per Serving

CALORIES	187
PROTEIN	9%
FAT	29% / 6.5 gm
CARBOHYDRATE	62%
SODIUM	93 mg

Desserts—Cookies

POPCORN BALLS

GRANDMOTHER'S HALVAH

POPCORN BALLS

2 cups brown rice syrup

¼ cup honey

2 tsp. vanilla

1 Tbs. molasses

1 tsp. butter flavored salt

3 gal. popped corn

1 cup dry roasted peanuts or sunflower seeds or pecans (opt.)

1. Mix together the popped popcorn and nuts in a large mixing bowl and set aside while you cook the syrup.

2. Place brown rice syrup, honey, vanilla molasses and salt in a saucepan and bring to a boil. Simmer for 10 - 15 minutes—use the "soft ball" test (with spoon, dribble a few drops of boiling mix in cold water. A ball should form, soft to the touch).

3. Quickly pour the hot liquid over the popcorn and nuts and mix lightly but thoroughly with a large spoon.

5. To make balls, spray hands with Pam and form handsful of the coated popcorn into balls by pressing together lightly into round balls.

Tip: ¾ cup un-popped corn yields 1 gallon popped corn.

Prep. time: 30 min.
Cooking time: 10 min.

Variation 1: Add ⅓ cup tahini or peanut butter to the cooked syrup just before pouring over the popcorn. A flavorful option, but higher in fat!

Variation 2:
(see picture p. 144)

CRUNCHY CLUSTERS

Instead of popped corn, use: 8 cups Kix cereal, 7 rice cakes (broken into pieces), 1 cup each: sesame seeds, slivered almonds, sunflower seeds

For step #5, press into circular molds or press entire mix firmly into oiled cookie sheet. Bake at 350° until golden brown (about 10 minutes - be careful, it burns easily). Scribe with knife into squares while still hot. Cool and break.

GRANDMOTHER'S HALVAH

2 cups sesame seeds

¼ cup carob powder

½ cup honey

1 Tbs. vanilla

1 tsp. salt

1. Place all ingredients in a food processor and blend until it forms a ball.

2. Press into a small flat pan or shallow, flat Rubbermaid storage container with lid.

3. Freeze and then cut in squares to serve. Keep it in your freezer for a perfect after-dinner dessert treat.

Prep. time: 15 min.

Makes 22 balls

Nutrient Information
Per Serving

CALORIES	192
PROTEIN	7%
FAT	18% / 3.9 gm
CARBOHYDRATE	75%
SODIUM	154 mg

Makes 12 - 15 pieces

Nutrient Information
Per Serving

CALORIES	195
PROTEIN	13%
FAT	57% / 14 gm
CARBOHYDRATE	30%
SODIUM	195 mg

PEANUTBUTTER CAROB PINWHEELS

LEMON SESAME CRISPS

PEANUTBUTTER CAROB PINWHEELS

1. Make a double Peanut Butter Cookie recipe through steps 1 and 2 (p. 147). Divide mix into two balls.

2. Place one ball into a bowl and work ½ cup carob powder into it with your hands. If your carob powder is a light color, add 1 tsp. Kitchen Bouquet to make it darker for contrast. You may need to add a small amount of water.

3. Roll out the first mix between 2 plastic bags that have been split open. Roll into a rectangle and remove top plastic to use again, leaving the dough on the bottom plastic.

5. Roll the second mix between two plastics to the same size rectangle as the first one. Remove top plastic and flip over onto the first rolled dough. Remove top plastic.

6. Roll up (in jelly-roll fashion) the two doughs together from the long edge, using the bottom plastic to help shape it as you go.

7. Slice ¼ inch slices and place on a cookie sheet. Bake at 350° for about 10 minutes until bottom is just beginning to brown and the top looks not quite browned. Cool on a rack.

Prep. time: 20 - 30 min.
Baking time: 10 min.

LEMON SESAME CRISPS

¼ cup tahini

2 Tbs. lemon flavor

2 tsp. vanilla

½ cup brown rice syrup

½ cup each: sesame seeds, sunflower seeds, coconut, quick oatmeal, oat bran, oat flour, fructose

½ tsp. salt

1. Mix together the first 4 ingredients and set aside.

2. Mix together in a mixing bowl the remaining ingredients; add liquid mix.

3. Scoop out onto a Pam-sprayed cookie sheet and bake at 350° for 10 minutes. Watch carefully— they should be lightly browned. Let cool before removing from pan with a metal spatula.

Prep. time: 15 min.
Baking time: 10 min.

Makes 24 cookies

Nutrient Information
Per Serving

CALORIES	155
PROTEIN	10%
FAT	41% / 8 gm
CARBOHYDRATE	49%
SODIUM	123 mg

Makes 16 cookies

Nutrient Information
Per Serving

CALORIES	284
PROTEIN	7%
FAT	38% / 13 gm
CARBOHYDRATE	55%
SODIUM	7 mg

COCONUT BARS

ALMOND JEWELS

COCONUT BARS

1 cup dates

2 cups water

¼ cup honey

3 cups un-sweetened coconut

3½ cups whole wheat pastry flour

1 cup white flour

2 cups quick oats

1½ cups Brazil Nut Butter

2 tsp. vanilla

2 tsp. salt

1. Blend dates, half the water and honey.

2. Meanwhile mix together all remaining ingredients except remaining water.

3. Stir in the date mixture and work with hands adding last cup of water as needed to make a moist though not sticky dough that can be rolled out.

4. Place on cookie sheet (two large ones needed) and cover with plastic wrap. Roll flat with a rolling pin to about ¼ inch thick.

5. Bake at 350° for about 20 minutes. Watch cookies at the edges of the pan and remove if they brown before the ones in the middle are finished baking.

Prep. time: 25 min.
Baking time: 20 - 30 min.

ALMOND JEWELS

¾ cup whole wheat pastry flour

¾ cup barley or unbleached wheat flour

1½ tsp. regular or 1 Tbs. Ener-G baking powder (opt.)

2 Tbs. cornstarch or tapioca flour or arrowroot

1 tsp. salt

½ cup almond or pecan butter

¾ cup Sucanat

¼ cup water

½ cup applesauce

1½ tsp. vanilla

1 cup Fresh Raspberry Jam (p. 87) or sugarless fruit spread

1. In a large bowl mix together the flours, baking powder, cornstarch and salt.

2. Work the almond butter into the flours with a pastry cutter or with your hands until evenly distributed.

3. Add Sucanat, apple-sauce, water, and vanilla. Stir until well mixed.

4. Place onto a cookie sheet with a small ice cream scoop or with two spoons. Make an inden-tation with the back of a spoon in the center of each cookie.

Tip: Dip spoon in water between each use.

5. Bake at 350° for about 15 minutes. Remove when the bottoms are just beginning to brown. Cool on a rack. Fill each depression with fruit filling.

Prep. time: 15 min.
Baking time: 15 min.

Makes 60 cookies

Nutrient Information
Per Serving
CALORIES	101
PROTEIN	9%
FAT	42% / 7 gm
CARBOHYDRATE	49%
SODIUM	73 mg

Makes 22 cookies

Nutrient Information
Per Serving
CALORIES	101
PROTEIN	9%
FAT	30% / 3.5 gm
CARBOHYDRATE	61%
SODIUM	100 mg

Desserts—Puddings and Fruit Desserts

A re you looking for the perfect way to top off a meal, leaving your guests satisfied without over-stuffing them with unneeded food? Try Tapioca Pudding. It's simple, and probably the dessert that more customers insist we keep in supply than any other we have served.

Photo key:

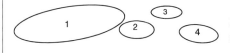

1. **Millet Pudding**
2. **Carob Pudding**
3. **Vanilla Pudding**
4. **Tapioca Pudding**

For a special occasion, combine pudding, cake, and fruit in an old fashioned English Trifle Cake. For a party, make Fruit Pizza your main course and serve popcorn and/or muffins with it.

CASHEW CHEESE CAKE

1 cup cashew nuts

1 cup water

½ cup honey (a light color of honey is best.)

2 Tbs. Emes Kosher Jel*

¾ cup pineapple juice

½ tsp. salt

¾ cup crushed pineapple (opt.)

Ice cubes or water to equal 1 quart total mixture

You may substitute 1 stick of agar for the Emes Jel. If using agar you will need to break up the stick of agar into the 1 cup of water and boil together for 1 full minute. Then blend as directed in Step #1.

This recipe may be frozen.

1. Place cashews, water and Emes Jel in a sauce pan and bring to a full boil. Blend about 2 minutes until smooth.

Makes 9" pie

Nutrient Information
Per Serving (⅛ pie)

CALORIES	305
PROTEIN	7%
FAT	36% / 13 gm
CARBOHYDRATE	57%
SODIUM	157 mg

Hint: Take care when blending very hot liquid as it can easily spray out when the blender starts. A towel draped over the blender should be used to hold the lid firmly in place. (The blending action of the blades in boiling hot liquid raises the internal vapor pressure and can very firmly blow off the lid especially when the blender is very full. Avoid serious burns—be careful!)

2. Add pineapple juice, salt, and enough ice cubes or water to equal 1 quart total mixture. Blend until smooth and then add the crushed pineapple. Blend only 2 or 3 seconds to chop more finely, but not to blend it smooth.

3. Pour into baked 9 inch Crumble Pie Crust, or double the recipe and pour into a 9 x 13 inch cake pan that has a Crumble Crust (p. 138) on the bottom. Chill 3 or 4 hours and serve with a fruit topping. Our favorite is Fresh Raspberry Jam (p. 87).

*Prep. time: 30 minutes
Chilling time: 4 hr.*

Variation: Try adding ½ lemon rind and 1 tsp. lemon extract in blender, step #1.

When making any blended pudding remember that the secret to success is in the blending. Be particular about smoothness and don't be impatient and satisfied to stop blending too soon. Stop the blender and take a tiny sample between your thumb and finger. Feel the creaminess of the sauce and keep blending until you no longer feel any graininess. Long blending will eventually bring the desired smoothness even if it takes 5 minutes. But be sure the mixture is swirling easily through the blades, forming a funnel or whirlpool in the center as it blends. If the mixture is too thick, it forms an air pocket around the blades and no efficient blending action is taking place. If this is happening, add more water, but not too much because a thick mixture will blend smooth more quickly than a very thin mixture. If you can't get a good action, you may have too much in your blender. Pour half of it out, and blend in portions.

TAPIOCA PUDDING*

1 cup blanched almonds**

1¼ cups hot water

¼ cup tapioca

1 tsp. vanilla

1 tsp. coconut extract

½ tsp. salt

⅓ cup honey or fruit juice sweetener

3 cups water

**You may use raw almonds with the skins on if you don't have blanched. Just cover with water and bring to a boil, drain and blend in Step #1. When they are strained in Step #2, the skins will remain in the cloth and the milk that you strain out will be just slightly darker than it is when you use blanched almonds.

Prep. time: 20 min.
Cooking time: 15 min.

*Courtesy of
Rilla Klingbeil

1. Blend almonds with hot water for about one minute. Add 3 cups water and blend briefly.

2. Place a cloth-lined sieve over a kettle and pour the blended almonds and water through the cloth. Close up cloth securely around the almond pulp and squeeze out as much of the water as you can. (Almond pulp can be saved and used in pie crust, granola, cookies, confections, loafs, bread, etc.)

3. Add remaining ingredients to almond milk in kettle and stir occasionally while bringing to a boil. When it is barely beginning to boil (steam is rising and first little bubble rises), remove from heat and place in shallow container to cool quickly in the refrigerator. Over-boiling will result in a less desirable thick and gummy consistency.

Hint: Altitude and humidity will affect the needed boiling time. While boiling too much gives a poor result, higher altitude or humidity will require more boiling, even as long as one full minute. It may take some experimenting to get it just right for your area. Too little boiling results in a pudding which is too runny.

4. An attractive serving idea is to layer the pudding in tall, glass dessert dishes with small spoonsful of Fresh Raspberry Jam (p. 87).

Makes 6 servings

Nutrient Information
Per Serving (¾ cup)

CALORIES	219
PROTEIN	8%
FAT	48% / 13 gm
CARBOHYDRATE	44%
SODIUM	mg

Desserts—Puddings and Fruit Desserts

MILLET PUDDING

VANILLA PUDDING

MILLET PUDDING

3 cups cooked millet (¾ cup millet cooked in 3½ cups water)

1½ cups pineapple juice

1 Tbs. lemon juice

¼ t. lemon extract(opt.)

1 tsp. salt

½ cup cashews

½ cup honey

1½ cups Grape Nuts cereal

3 to 4 cups fresh or frozen fruit (raspberries, strawberries, bananas, peaches, blueberries or other fruit of choice)

2 cups Granola (p. 17)

1. Blend hot millet with juices, cashews, honey and flavorings in blender until very smooth—it may take about 2 minutes.

Unless you have a very strong blender, you might need to blend just half a recipe at a time. If blending all at once, use a rubber spatula to stir the top portion in as it blends, but do it carefully so as not to catch spatula in blender blades!

2. Place a layer of Grape Nuts cereal in the bottom of a 9 x 13 inch glass dish. Gently pour half the pudding over the cereal, then add a layer of berries or other fruit of choice, the rest of the pudding, and finally end with a layer of granola on the top. Chill 3 or 4 hours before serving to let it firm up.

Tip: Be sure to use freshly cooked, hot millet. Left over millet that has been heated up doesn't firm up very well when cooled.

Hint: Several spoonfuls of Fresh Raspberry Jam (p. 87) drizzled here and there in this dish makes it very attractive and delicious!

VANILLA PUDDING OR PIE FILLING

⅓ cup cashew pieces

½ cup cooked, hot rice

⅓ cup honey or fruit juice sweetener

¼ tsp. salt

1 tsp. vanilla

5 Tbs. flour or 4 Tbs. cornstarch

2½ cups water

1. Place all ingredients in blender with just 1½ cups of the water and blend until very smooth—at least 1 minute. Add remaining 1 cup of water at the end.

2. Place in a sauce pan and bring to a boil, stirring constantly. Pour immediately into pie or pizza crusts, or into container for chilling.

Uses: This makes a very good filling for banana cream pie, layering in a pre-baked crust with bananas. Also a good filling for tortes and fruit pizza. One recipe fills one pie or a 12 inch fruit pizza.

Prep. time: 10 min.
Cooking time: 10 min.

Makes 12 servings

Nutrient Information
Per Serving (½ cup)

CALORIES	213
PROTEIN	7%
FAT	13% / 3.5 gm
CARBOHYDRATE	80%
SODIUM	214 mg

Vanilla Pudding
Makes 4 servings
Nutrient Information
Per Serving (¾ cup)

CALORIES	216
PROTEIN	5%
FAT	22% / 5.6 gm
CARBOHYDRATE	73%
SODIUM	137 mg

Desserts—Puddings and Fruit Desserts

KIMBERLEY'S TRIFLE CAKE

PLAIN CAKE

KIMBERLEY'S TRIFLE CAKE

This is definitely a special occasion dessert to make for a group or take to a potluck. It is not at all difficult to make if you plan ahead. The Lemon Chiffon Pudding has to be made several hours ahead—it needs to set up and then be re-blended. Some substitutions can be made for a simpler version, such as, make just a double recipe of one of the puddings, or just use Millet Pudding. Any fruit sauce will do in place of the Raspberry Jam.

So, here's what you need:

1 Plain Cake (this page) cut in 1 inch cubes

4 cups Fresh Raspberry Jam (p. 87)

1 recipe Tapioca Pudding (p.153)

1 recipe Lemon Chiffon Pie (p. 141)

In deep, straight-sided glass bowl assemble in layers in order as follows:

1. Two Peaches, nectarines, or apricots sliced thinly in wedges (may use canned if out of season). Arrange along bottom and sides so they will show.

2. Half of cake cut in 1 inch cubes

3. 2 cups Fresh Raspberry Jam

4. All of the tapioca pudding

5. 2 peaches, nectarines or apricots sliced

6. Second half of cake cut in 1 inch cubes

7. 2 cups Raspberry Jam

8. All of the Creamy Lemon Chiffon Pie filling

9. Chill 2 hr. or overnight

Note: The Chiffon Pudding must be re-blended and poured over the top. But since it sets up very quickly after blending, be ready to quickly pour over the top of the "cake."

Sometimes it can be too thick. If it seems rubbery instead of soft and almost ready to lose its shape, add some milk or more coconut nectar when re-blending.

*Prep. time: 2 hr.
Chilling time: 2 hr., or overnight*

PLAIN CAKE

1 cup applesauce

¾ cup fruit juice sweetener (or ½ cup honey and ¼ cup water)

⅔ cup water

2 cups white pastry or cake flour

1 cup whole wheat pastry flour

3 Tbs. Ener-G Baking Powder (or alternate)

1 tsp. salt

Mix together and quickly pour into a sprayed 9 x 13 inch cake pan. Bake about 25 minutes at 350° or until just getting brown on top.

*Prep. time: 10 min.
Baking time: 25 min.*

Makes 20 servings

Nutrient Information
Per Serving

CALORIES	167
PROTEIN	6%
FAT	27% / gm
CARBOHYDRATE	67%
SODIUM	99 mg

Makes 12 servings

Nutrient Information
Per Serving

CALORIES	159
PROTEIN	9%
FAT	3% / .4 gm
CARBOHYDRATE	88%
SODIUM	180 mg

WHIPPED TOPPING**

1¼ cups water

2 Tbs. Emes gelatin (unflavored)

1 - 14 oz. can coconut milk

½ cup cashew nuts*

½ cup honey or fructose

2 Tbs. powdered lecithin granules (opt. see below)

1¼ Tbs. lemon juice

½ tsp. salt

½ tsp. vanilla

½ tsp. coconut extract

1 cup tofu

This is the only recipe in the entire book which lists "free fat" in the ingredients. The result is quite acceptable without the lecithin, though not as creamy, smooth or "whipped-cream like." For the most healthful plan, leave it out but if you have a visitor or other acquaintance who isn't very interested in healthful things, this might be a reasonable transition from dairy items towards more healthful products.

1. Bring water and Emes Kosher Jel to a boil.

2. Place in blender along with remaining ingredients and blend for 2 minutes.

3. Pour into a flat casserole and chill until set.

4. Before serving, whip vigorously with a wire whip or briefly with an electric beater (not too long with the beater, or it will be runny).

5. Return to refrigeraor and chill, or serve right away.

Hint: This cream will keep in the refrigerator for a week so make it ahead and keep it handy as a nice touch for your desserts. Excellent on Pumpkin, Lemon, Keylime pie, or Apple Crisp.

Tip: Can be frozen; thaw at room temp. and whip.

Hint: Cannot be used on hot desserts—it will melt!

Prep. time: 15 min.
Cooking time: 5 min.

*For lower fat version, cashews may be left out

**Courtesy of Rilla Klingbeil

Makes 5 cups

Nutrient Information
Per Serving (2 Tbs.)

CALORIES	57
PROTEIN	11%
FAT	59% / 4 gm
CARBOHYDRATE	30%
SODIUM	141 mg

CAROB PUDDING

1 cup cooked rice

¼ cup cashews or ½ cup tofu

2 cups water

2 Tbs. Emes Kosher Jel

½ cup date pieces

2 Tbs. prune sauce or 4 soft pitted prunes

⅓ cup conc. fruit sweetener or ¼ cup honey

¼ tsp. vanilla

½ tsp. salt

½ tsp. coconut extract

½ tsp. Roma or Pero

⅛ tsp. almond extract

¼ cup carob powder

1. Place cashews (or tofu), rice, dates, and water in a saucepan and bring to a boil.

2. Place hot rice mixture in blender along with Emes Kosher Jel. Place lid on blender and cover with a towel to protect from any hot liquid coming out when you turn it on.

3. Turn on blender and blend for at least 2 minutes while adding the remaining ingredients.

4. Pour hot pudding into a container and refrigerate for several hours until chilled.

5. May be used as is, or for a lighter pudding, place in blender and blend again to aerate. Pour into a bowl and chill.

Hint: This makes a perfect topping for Carob Prune Cake. Spread over the top of the cooled cake after re-blending and chill for at least 1 hour before serving.

Chilling time: 2 hr. plus

Makes 4 cups

Nutrient Information
Per Serving (2/3 cups)

CALORIES	180
PROTEIN	5%
FAT	14% / gm
CARBOHYDRATE	81%
SODIUM	181 mg

BLENDER ICE CREAM

FRUIT SHAKES

BLENDER ICE CREAM

1 cup cashew nuts or blanched almonds

½ cup soft or chopped dates

½ cup honey

½ tsp. salt

2 tsp. vanilla

4 cups water

1. Place all ingredients in the blender with 2 cups of the water. Blend for about 2 minutes until very smooth.

2. Add remaining 2 cups of water and pour about 1 inch deep into cake pans or similar. Place in freezer overnight.

3. When ready to serve, or about 1 hr. before, remove from freezer, cut in squares that can be blended easily.

Variation: For a creamier and more nutritious ice cream, add 1½ cups cooked brown rice (blend entire mix very smooth)

4. Place ¾ cup water in blender and add about ½ of the frozen squares, one at a time while they blend. Keep adding frozen squares until the consistency of soft ice cream. Pour out and store in freezer for about an hour if necessary until ready to use. Repeat with ¾ cup water and remaining frozen squares.

Tip: Frozen bananas may be added for variation of flavor and sweetness. But be sure to freeze them when ripe—nicely speckled, but not overripe. Peel and cut banana in several pieces and place in freezer for future use.

Prep. time: 15 min.
Chill: 4 hr. or overnight

FRUIT SHAKES

1 cup frozen fruits of choice, such as:
  Strawberries
  Bananas cut in 1 inch pieces
  Blueberries
  Blackberries
  Raspberries
  Mangoes
  Peaches
  Cherries
1 cup Blender Ice Cream* or frozen banana pieces

¼ cup apple juice conc. or 2 Tbs. honey

½ cup or more liquid (water or juice or milk)

1. Place fruit, Ice Cream, and juice or honey in blender and turn on.

2. If your ingredients are frozen solid, you may need to add ½ cup or more liquid for a blend which keeps moving through the blades. Add more liquid or frozen fruit to make a thick shake. Adjust to your taste, depending on the tartness of the fruit.

3. Pour into shake glasses and serve, or place in freezer until ready to serve.

*Make plenty of Blender Ice Cream "cubes" and after it freezes (see step #2), take out and cut in squares and keep in plastic bags in freezer for using in shakes or ice cream.

Prep. time: 10 min.
Makes approx. 4 cups

Makes 8 cups

Nutrient Information
Per Serving (½ cup)

CALORIES	101
PROTEIN	6%
FAT	32% / gm
CARBOHYDRATE	62%
SODIUM	69 mg

Makes 4 servings

Nutrient Information
Per Serving (1 cup)

CALORIES	122
PROTEIN	4%
FAT	14% / 10 gm
CARBOHYDRATE	82%
SODIUM	44 mg

Desserts—Puddings and Fruit Desserts

HOMEMADE ICE CREAM

HOMEMADE ICE CREAM

2 quarts soy milk

½ cup cashew nuts

1 whole medium (not large) banana (yellow—not green or spotted!)

1 - 10 ½ oz. pkg. boxed tofu (Mori-nu or similar—these "boxed" tofus seem to be more mild in flavor)

1 - 12 oz. can frozen apple juice conc.

1/8 tsp. salt

vanilla to taste

1½ cup fresh or frozen berries, (opt.)

2 tsp. guar gum or xanthan gum (opt.—to give more body and texture without added fat!)

1. Place cashew nuts in blender and add a small amount of the milk, just enough to blend the cashews smooth. Blend for about 2 minutes, until mixture is very creamy and not at all grainy. Add tofu and banana and more of the milk, salt, and vanilla, and blend again until smooth. Pour into 1 gallon ice cream freezing container.

2. Place thawed apple juice in blender along with half of the frozen, thawed berries. Blend smooth and add to the milk mixture in the freezing container along with the remaining berries which you should cut up into little pieces.

Hint: If you want to make vanilla ice cream, omit the berries and just add the apple juice (or use another sweetener of your choice such as brown rice syrup, fruit juice sweetener, or blended dates and honey).

3. Fill the container up to the 1 gallon mark with soy milk and put in the blades and lid. Mix according to the directions of your ice cream freezer. Serve and eat as soon as it freezes.

Makes 16 servings

Nutrient Information
Per Serving (1 cup)
CALORIES	143
PROTEIN	19%
FAT	36% / 6 gm
CARBOHYDRATE	45%
SODIUM	41 mg

SMOOTHIES

SMOOTHIES

⅓ cup apple juice

½ cup frozen strawberries

1 frozen banana

1. Break banana into 4 inch pieces and place in blender with the juice.

2. Blend smooth—adding strawberries one by one. Serve in tall glasses.

Makes 2 servings

Nutrient Information
Per Serving (1 cup)
CALORIES	91
PROTEIN	4%
FAT	4% / 0 gm
CARBOHYDRATE	92%
SODIUM	2 mg

159

BREAKING THE FAST

Bavarian Breakfast

Muesli
Pumpkin Muffins with Orange Marmalade
Grapefruit

Energy Breakfast

Granola with Cashew-Rice Milk and raisins
Whole Wheat Toast with Fresh Raspberry Jam
2 whole fruits in season *(apple, orange, banana, cantaloupe)*

Sunday Morning Brunch

Sunday Brunch Waffles
Blueberry Sauce
Blender Ice Cream
Fresh fruit in season

Hungry Farmer Breakfast

Scrambled Tofu
Hash Brown Potato Patties
Whole Wheat Toast with Millet Butter and Honey
Fresh fruit in season

Winter Morning Special

No-Fail Oatmeal with raisins or dates
Banana-Nut Muffins
Cup of hot carob drink
Citrus Medley *(Oranges and Grapefruit cut up with juice)*

MENUS

Family Favorite
Crepes
Strawberry or Apple Filling
Fresh fruit in season

Sabbath Morning Delight
Blueberry Fruit Toast
Fresh fruit in season

Sabbath Surprise
Millet Pudding
Whole Wheat Toast with Peanut Butter and fruit spread
Fresh Fruit in season

DINING LIKE A KING
Holiday Flair
Pecan Loaf with Brown Gravy
Bread Dressing
Creamed Potatoes and Peas
Cranberry Strawberry Mold
Pumpkin Pie

Christmas Eve Buffet
Zucchini Quiche Tarts *(Veggie Quiche)*
Armenian Lentil Soup
Relish Tray and Crackers with Sliceable Cashew Cheese
Fruit Bread Wreath and Millet Butter
Apple Crisp

MENUS

Make Ahead Fiesta
Enchilada Frijoles
Corn on the Cob with Millet Butter or Fiesta Corn
(Frozen corn with red and green peppers)
Cucumber Salad

Mexican Summer Family Pleaser
Taco Salad—Corn chips or rice served as a base and piled with
Chili, diced tomatoes, shredded lettuce, sliced olives and diced
onions all topped with salsa and Tahini Cheese or
Tofu Sour Cream or Guacamole
Corn Muffins

Italian Cuisine
Stuffed Manicotti or Lasagna
Steamed Broccoli
Tossed Salad with Italian Dressing
Whole Wheat French Bread with Millet Butter

Italian Traditions
Spaghetti and Pasta Sauce
Tofu Walnut Balls or Spinach-Tofu Balls
Tossed Salad with Greek Olive Dressing
Spinach Cheese Toast

Simple and Hearty
Cuban Black Beans on Brown Rice
Coleslaw or Stuffed Tomatoes with Tofu Cottage Cheese
Whole wheat bread or rolls with Millet Butter

MENUS

Sabbath Make-Ahead Dinner
Cashew-Carrot Loaf *(Make in Bundt pan)*
Easy Chicken-Like Gravy
Mashed Potatoes *(make a day ahead and warm in oven or micro to serve)*
Steamed Broccoli Tips Au Gratin
Whole wheat rolls with Millet Butter and Fruit Spread
Key lime Pie

Sabbath Dinner Too
Pasta Primavera
Steamed Brussel Sprouts with Tofu Sour Cream
Tossed Salad with Creamy Cucumber Dressing
Whole Wheat French Bread with Millet Butter
Carob Prune Cake

Russian Winter
Chunky Vegetable Soup *(Borscht)*
Caraway Rye Bread with Cheese Too Spread
Russian Potato Salad
Coconut Bars

From the Garden
Oatburgers with Brown Gravy
Baked Red Potatoes
Zucchini Creole
Bread or Rolls with Millet Butter

Springtime Favorite
Creamed Asparagus over toast or long grain brown rice
Carrot and Raisin Salad

MENUS

Simple—But Sensational
Tofu Walnut Balls
Quinoa Pilaf *(Make Quinoa and add some diced steamed vegetables like carrots, peas, cauliflower, and onions)*
Thai Peanut Sauce *(serve over Walnut Balls and Quinoa)*
Tossed Salad with French Dressing
Bread with Millet Butter

Friday Dinner
Chili
Baked Potatoes with Tofu Sour Cream
Winter Fruit Salad
Toast with Avocado slices and onion salt

Picnic at Home
Vegeburgers
French Fries
Ketchup Spread for Fries
Strawberry-Banana Fruit Shakes

LUNCHTIME FARE
Sack Lunch for Mom
Veggie Sandwich Spread Sandwich
Carrot and Celery Sticks
Pineapple Date Bars

School Lunch Box
Peanut butter, creamed honey, and banana sandwich
Almonds and Dried Bananas
Red Delicious Apple

MENUS

Lunch Break at Work
Falafil Pocket Sandwich
(tomatoes and lettuce or sprouts in a baggie with Hummus or Spread in a small container to be stuffed into the pocket at lunch time.)
Four Bean Salad
Oatmeal Raisin Cookies

Box Lunch Banquet
Tofu Walnut Balls *(with Ketchup Spread)*
Steamed Asparagus Spears *(hot or cold)*
Couscous Salad
Apple Turnovers
Martinelli Sparkling Apple Juice

Shopping Day Car Lunch
Hot Corn Chowder in a thermos
Rye Krisp and Avocado slices or Guacamole
Banana Date Cookies

Picnic at the Park
Hickory Burgers
Potato Salad or Fat Free Potato Chips
Carrot Cake

Salad Picnic
Vegetable Medley Salad
Cucumber Salad
Bread and Rye Krisp with Bean Spread
Pumpkin Pie

APPENDIX

Some of the recipes in this book will likely call for items that are unfamiliar to you. This section is a description of many of the ingredients used in this book with suggestions of where to buy them or what substitutes you might use. A few of our ingredients can be purchased only in restaurant or bakery supply stores It would be worth your effort sometime to look in the yellow pages and visit a "Cash and Carry" restaurant supply found in most cities. Or ask your local health food store or natural food co-op to stock things you can't find.

Agar Agar (or kanten)

Pronounced "AH-ger." Comes from the algae "agar-agar." It is rich in calcium, iron, phosphorus, and vitamins. Used mainly as a thickener, agar is an excellent vegan substitute for gelatin, which is an animal product. Far superior to traditional gelatin, which offers few health benefits, it can be used in much the same way that gelatin is used. It comes in several forms—flakes, powder, or sticks, or bundles of strands. Available in most Asian food stores or natural food stores, but is likely to cost more in a natural food store. 1 stick agar = 3 Tbs. (2 oz.) agar flakes = 3 tsp. agar powder=24 strands.

Almonds

Nutritionally, almonds are superior to cashews and peanuts. Its good to have plenty of raw almonds on hand for milks and sauces. Almond butter is very good and simple to make in a food processor. Raw almonds can be blanched by bringing to a boil and then rinsing in cold water—then slip the skins off while wet by squeezing between the thumb and finger.

Apple juice concentrate

Frozen apple juice concentrate is used in many of our recipes to replace sugar. It's a good idea to buy it by the case when it's on sale and keep on hand in your freezer. Restaurant supply stores carry an apple juice concentrate that is twice as concentrated as that found in the super market—a nice way to sweeten certain things without adding as much

liquid, but the recipes in this book are made with the kind you find in local supermarkets.

Baking Powder, Ener-G

Made simply of calcium carbonate and citric acid. Use it in proportions about 2 times that of regular baking powder and bake soon after mixing as the rising begins as soon as it is mixed. Carried in some natural food stores, but you will probably have to order it by mail. Ener-G Foods, Inc., P.O. Box 24723, Seattle, WA. 98124, (206) 767-6660

Baking Powder, Featherweight

Carried in many natural food stores, this one contains no aluminum or baking soda. Use it in proportions 1½ times that of regular baking powder. This, like Ener-G, is single-acting and has to be baked soon after mixing as the rising begins when mixed.

Baking Powder, Rumford

This baking powder is preferable to regular baking powders in that it is aluminum-free though it does contain baking soda which is objectionable to some.

Basil

Can be used freely in Italian dishes and sauces.

Bulgar wheat

Precooked and dried cracked wheat. Gives a meaty texture to some of our entrees.

Bernard Jensen's Instant Gravy Seasoning

A very flavorful seasoning in powdered form made from hydrolyzed plant protein. It gives things a meaty taste, but if you can't find it in your natural foods store, it can be substituted in the recipe with extra salt or soy sauce.

Bragg's Liquid Aminos

Made from soy beans, is similar to soy sauce, but not as strong and not fermented. It is sold in health food stores. For more information write: Live Food Products, Inc., box 7, Santa Barbara, CA 93102.

APPENDIX

Brown Rice Syrup

This cultured product is made from brown rice, water, and a small amount of natural cereal enzyme. The light and delicate syrup is about half as sweet as sugar.

Cardamom and Coriander

This Herb can be used combined to give desserts a spicy flavor similar to cinnamon, an irritating substance we have all learned to love but should avoid.

Carob powder

Made from the locust pod, carob powder has a fat content of 2% as compared to chocolate's 52%. It is high in calcium, phosphorus, potassium, iron, magnesium and other minerals and vitamins. Tastes enough like chocolate to be used as a "substitute." It is not bitter and therefore requires less sugar than chocolate to make it sweet. All brands of cocoa from which chocolate is made, contain more tannin per cup than tea which has approximately two grains per cup. Caffeine and theobromine (a cousin alkaloid to caffeine) may cause headaches, central nervous system irritation, general or localized itching, depression and anxiety. Caffeine content per cup of cocoa beverage is low (27 cups of chocolate drink to "equal" a cup of brewed coffee—see table below). Carob contains no tannin, caffeine, or theobromine. May be purchased from most natural food stores.

Caffeine content in mg/cup

Brewed coffee	137
Instant coffee	63
Black tea	47
Cocacola	33
Chololate milk	7
Chocolate drink	5

Cashew nuts

Cashews are seen in many vegan recipes because they are a soft nut and blend very smooth. This cashew paste can be used in many ways to take the place of milk, butter, and fat in recipes. Since they are not packed very clean, they should be washed or boiled before using in any uncooked recipes.

Chuka Soba

Found in oriental stores, these precooked noodles made of wheat take very little cooking and are very nice in soups, chow mein, or other dishes calling for Ramen or high-fat noodles fried in oil.

Cilantro

An herb used in Mexican food.

Coconut

Unsweetened shredded coconut is what we use in most of our cooking. It is usually only found in natural food stores or co-ops.

Clear Jel, Instant

Cornstarch in reality, but made from a hybrid waxy corn, this starch has a modified molecular structure and is pre-cooked to thicken upon contact with cold liquid. It should be blended rather than stirred into your preparation—it's an excellent way to thicken cold fruit sauces (doesn't work with heat). Some natural food stores carry it, but it's one of those items that is usually found only at a bakery supply or wholesale grocers' outlet in 25 lb. bags. Buy and share, or ask your natural food store to carry it.

Clear Jel, Regular

Very similar to the instant version though not pre-cooked (looks just like cornstarch), this has to be heated to become thick. It is superior to cornstarch for cooked fruit sauces because it retains its silky, smooth texture, hot or cold, whereas cornstarch-thickened sauces become jelly-like when cooled, or if then stirred, have a rough texture. Bakers use this for jelly-roll fillings or cheesecake toppings for that beautiful satin look. We like to can blueberries in season thickened with Clear Jel and sweetened with fruit sweetener. Then they're ready to use for Fruit Pizzas or turnovers.

Coconut milk

Comes in 10 oz. cans and may be found in the Asian section of a supermarket, or in Asian stores.

APPENDIX

Corn flour

Finely ground corn makes a nice binding agent in roasts and patties to take the place of eggs.

Cornmeal

We use yellow because we like the nice yellow color and flavor, but white cornmeal is equally nutritious.

Corn tortillas, see Tortilla

Dates

Date pieces coated with oat flour are very handy for cooking and baking. Dates of any shape can be used, but if dry and hard you should rinse them with water and leave in an airtight container several hours, or for quick use, boil them. They can be found in most natural food sections, or purchased at bakery supply stores in 25 or 30 lb.. They're much cheaper this way and can be divided into smaller amounts and frozen.

Do-pep: see Gluten Flour

Emes Kosher Jel

All our recipes use the unflavored gelatin. Pronounced "M-s," it is a vegetable gelatin product made from carageenan (from seaweed). Ordinary gelatin generally contains animal products, often including those considered "unclean" in the Bible. Ellen White's statements about the time coming when all animal products would be unsafe take on rather interesting significance considering the BSE scare in Europe. The prions (protien fragment) which cause this disease are not "living" material and require 700° Celcius (1,300° Fahrenheit) to be destroyed! This is far above the temperature used in rendering plants where the "purified" gelatin constituents are sometimes produced.

One special characteristic of a recipe made with Emes is that it can be re-blended it after it is chilled and set up to give an aerated, lighter quality to the dessert. One disadvantage is that it has to be chilled to stay "set-up." If left out at room temperature it will get soft and lose its shape. Found in some natural food stores, and in the health food section of many Adventist Book Centers, call 1-800-235-3000 for the ABC nearest you. If you don't mind using an animal product, Knox Unflavored Gelatin may be substituted.

Flour

It is best to keep all flours in the refrigerator or freezer to preserve their freshness. Wherever possible we use flours other than wheat in our cookies, muffins, and pie crusts—partly for variety of nutrition and also because we have so many customers who are allergic to wheat or cannot tolerate gluten. Most of these flours and grains will have to be purchased from a natural food store or co-op.

Fructose (50% sweeter than sugar)

Used in a few of the dessert recipes where extra sweetening is needed without extra liquid. Refined from fruit and sweeter than sucrose but nutritionally little better.

Fruit juice sweetener

This is now used by many bakeries and food manufacturers to replace sugar, and can be found in most natural food stores. It is usually made from peach, pear, and pineapple concentrates combined. Mystic Lake Fruit Sweetener is a widely distributed brand, but Tree Top makes one that seems to be available through bakery suppliers. Its sweetening effect is superior to apple juice concentrate in most recipes because it is has a milder, less acidic taste.

Garbanzos

Sometimes called chick peas these are found in almost any supermarket.

Garlic powder

If you can find granulated garlic, which is more coarse than garlic powder, you will find it mixes better in hot soups and sauces without clumping.

Gelatin, see Emes Kosher Jel

Gluten flour or Do-pep

It is derived from whole wheat and is the glutenous part of the grain that causes bread to be light and elastic. It is high in protein, and is not needed for nutrition, but is helpful as a binder or adding to flour that has a low gluten content when making bread.

Gums

Xanthan gum or guar gum are generally found in most health food stores and are used as substitutes for fat in many commercial products to mimic its texture.

Honey

Used sparingly in some of our recipes because the result in the body is basically the same as sugar.

Italian seasoning

Nice combination of herbs.

Kitchen Bouquet

Comes in a bottle like soy sauce, but much darker. Made of caramelized sugars and vegetables. Good for giving certain foods a rich brown color. Can be found in the seasoning section of most super markets.

Lecithin

A thick, viscous oily paste (sometimes prepared as dried granules and often available at Fred Meyers). We use lecithin to treat baking sheets and pans. Spread a thin film on the pan with a paper towel—it provides a very effective non-stick coating that lasts through several bakings with very little fat being absorbed into the food.

Lemon juice

Pure fresh or frozen is superior, but reconstituted bottled lemon juice also works in all our recipes.

Liquid Aminos, see Bragg's

Manicotti

A pasta shaped like a hollow tube which you stuff and bake. Found in supermarkets.

McKay's Chicken Seasoning

This chicken-like seasoning contains no animal fat and is found in most natural food stores, and on request can be ordered without MSG, white pepper or whey.

Millet, whole

Similar to rice, but needs more water than rice for cooking.

Non-stick spray

Pam is a familiar brand, but many others are now on the market including one made of olive oil. Very handy for giving a quick, thin non-stick coating to pans or waffle irons.

Nutritional Yeast, see Yeast

Nuts

The more common nuts and seeds can be purchased at your supermarket or natural food store, but to save money go to a co-op, or buy them bulk wholesale from a bakery supply. By looking in the Yellow Pages under "Nuts-wholesale", you will find places in most cities that will sell to you 25 or 30 lb. cases or tins of nuts or dried fruits at a real savings. Share or divide and freeze.

Oat flour

Can be purchased or make your own by blending 2 cups of oatmeal in the blender until fine.

Oatmeal

Oatmeal is simply oats that have been rolled flat in a special steam process. Quick oatmeal is the same as Old Fashioned rolled oats—just cut up in smaller pieces.

Onions, dehydrated

These can be found in the seasoning section of your supermarket, but if bought in a small bottle they can be expensive. Look for larger containers in the larger wholesale stores such Cosco or a Cash and Carry if you happen to have one in your area. They are so handy to use and give a toasty onion flavor to any recipe. During most seasons of the year, it is cheaper to use dehydrated onions than

APPENDIX

fresh ones, so here is one way to save both money and time. But if you don't have them, you can easily substitute a raw diced onion or onion powder in any recipe.

Onion powder

A great flavor we use freely in soups, entree, and sauces. Granulated onion is easier to mix into a hot liquid than onion powder since it is more coarse, but onion powder has a superior delicate flavor.

Peanuts

Dry roasted, unsalted peanuts are the ones we use and can be found in many supermarkets, but less expensive to buy in bulk from a wholesale outlet or co-op. For the sake of freshness we make our own peanut butter out of these nuts in a food processor.

Potato flour

This is pre-cooked dried potatoes ground into flour. Therefore, it is great for thickening anything without cooking, but is best to add it in the blender for a smooth product. Usually found in natural food stores, but check the ingredients to be sure it is potato flour and not potato starch which is like cornstarch and has to be cooked to thicken.

Red peppers

Red Bell Peppers, fresh or canned, make soups, salads and entrees look very special. Restaurant supply stores have canned, diced red peppers in larger cans, making them very economical. Unused portions can be frozen.

Rice

We prefer the long grain brown rice because of its fluffy appearance and texture when cooked. Short grain is just as nutritious.

Rice flour

We use the brown rice flour in several recipes. If you don't have it on hand, you can make your own by blending 2 cups of brown rice until fine in the blender.

Salt, Butter Flavored

We use it to give Millet Butter the right flavor. Shilling's makes a nicely flavored one that can be found in most super markets, but

certain popcorn salts will do just as well and are less expensive.

Savory

Good in soups.

Sesame seeds

They can be purchased either raw or blanched. We use the blanched for better flavor and color and since they are usually used only as a garnish, there is no advantage to using the less appealing raw ones.

Sesame Tahini

Tahini is sesame seeds ground to butter. It is very unsatisfactory to make your own in a food processor or blender since they are too tiny to blend smooth. Joyva brand tahini is the best we have found for flavor—it is more mild and has a less bitter taste than most other brands of tahini. We use it in a few recipes to take the place of refined oils.

Soy sauce

Most soy sauce is manufactured using fermentation processes, so we prefer not to use it. Some brands are fermentation free and if you compare the taste and smell you'll detect the difference.

Soy Spaghetti

Spaghetti made with soy flour and more nutritious than enriched spaghetti. Found in natural food stores.

Spelt spaghetti or macaroni

Found in many natural food stores this whole grain pasta is superior to whole wheat pasta in the way it cooks and keeps its shape when cooked. Gives a delightful wholesome flavor to your pasta dishes.

Spinach spaghetti

Durum spaghetti with spinach added to the pasta. It is a lively color and more nutritious than plain enriched spaghetti. This is carried by some supermarkets or natural food.

Sucanat

Short for "sugar cane natural," Sucanat is made by processing the juice from sugar cane, and then dehydrating it.

Sunflower seeds

Raw unsalted sunflower seeds can be easily found in most natural food stores or co-ops, and are less expensive than other nuts. Therefore, you might use them in some recipes calling for cashews where color or texture doesn't matter.

Tofu

Made from soy bean curd, this can be found in the produce section of most supermarkets. It will keep better after purchased by opening the plastic cover and draining off the water, then keep in a container covered with fresh water and change the water every day or two.

Tortillas, corn, soft, uncooked

These may be purchased in the refrigerator or freezer section of many supermarkets (or make your own—see our Lefse recipe, p. 115). There are two kinds—thick or thin. We prefer the thick ones for enchiladas, and the thin ones for soft tacos.

Turmeric

Mainly used to give a yellow color to certain recipes such as scrambled Tofu and Mustard Spread

Vanilla

We like to use white vanilla powder in certain desserts and our Non-dairy ice cream. You will find it in most supermarkets or in restaurant and bakery supply stores. It contains no alcohol and doesn't darken a white dessert.

Vege-Sal

A very nice vegetable seasoning that is handy to use when you're making any savory dish that needs more flavor, but you're not sure what it needs. Found in natural food stores.

Vegetable pasta spirals

Found in most supermarkets or natural food stores these are more nutritious than enriched pasta and add a nice color to salads.

Vita-burger or TVP

A dry burger-like food made from soy. It is nice in chili or some other dishes to give a meaty texture.

White flour, Unbleached

Better to use than the regular bleached white flour to avoid the chemicals used in bleaching, but still has much of the nutrition removed. We use it in small amounts in some desserts to give a lighter texture, also in some pastries or breads combined with whole wheat flour.

Whole-wheat flour

For bread making, look for a high-protein "hard" wheat flour. It has a higher gluten content for lighter raised baked goods.

Whole Wheat Lasagna

Look for this in natural food stores.

Whole-wheat pastry flour

Best for pastry or other non-yeast baked products because it is made from "soft" wheat and has a lower gluten content, making your cakes and pastries more tender.

Wright's Hickory Seasoning

We use to give some foods, such as Split Pea Soup and Hickory Burgers, a wood-grilled taste. It can be purchased from the seasoning section of most super markets.

Xanthan Gum

See Gum

Yeast, Active Dry

We use Saf-Instant, an instant type yeast that doesn't have to be dissolved in warm water before mixing, but can be added right to the dough in the first stages of mixing. If you can't find this brand, Red Star and Fleichman's are good and available in most super markets. You save money by buying it in a 1 pound package and storing the unused portion in your freezer.

Yeast flakes, Nutritional

Good nutritional yeast flakes are yellow and have a gentle cheese-like flavor. This product is similar to brewer's yeast but has a less bitter taste. Some brands have whey in the formula, so you have to read labels carefully if you want to avoid this dairy by-product.

TOPICAL SECTION INDEX

TOPICAL SECTION INDEX

TOPICAL SECTION INDEX

INDEX

INDEX

INDEX

INDEX

INDEX

INDEX

Special CHIP Insert

BARBECUED TOFU

1. Freeze 2 lbs. firm tofu, thaw, squeeze out and cut in 1" X 3" strips:

2. Mix together in blender until smooth:

½ cup peanut butter

1 T. paprika

4 T. water

½ t. garlic pawder

1 ½ t. salt

3. Pour into flat bowl. Dip tofu in blended mixture. Let cook in oven about 20 minutes before adding sauce. Brown both sides.

SAUCES

In kettle put all of the following ingredients:

1 medium onion

2 cloves garlic, minced

1 quart tomatoes

1 c. tomato paste

3 T. honey

1 ½ T. molasses

1 ½ t. salt

1 ½ t. dried parsley

May add oregano, basil, and cumin to taste if desired. Bring to boil, reduce heat and simmer for at least an hour. Add 1 T. lemon juice and 2 T. Braggs liquid aminos.

Pour over tofu strips and bake until liquid has thickened.

CHEESE SAUCE

1 ½ cup raw cashew pieces

2 cup hot water

1 cup pimento

1   tsp. salt

3 Tbsp. food yeast flakes

1 ½ cups hot cooked millet

1 Tbsp. lemon juice

1 potato, cooked and hot

1. Blend cashews in water until smooth.

2. Add seasonings, pimiento and millet water. Continue to blend.

3. Add potato and blend until very smooth.

4. Serve hot or cold over vegetables, pizza, lasagna, macaroni, baked potatoes, etc.

PECAN PIE

1 cup boiling water

1 cup pecans

1 teaspoon salt

2 teaspoons vanilla

1 cup soy milk powder

1 teaspoon butterscotch

2/3 cup real maple syrup

1 1/4 teaspoon agar powder

1. Mix soy milk powder and water in blender.

2. Add other ingredients except nuts (salt, vanilla, butterscotch, maple syrup Agar powder):

3. Pour mixture into pie shell and arrange nuts over the top

4. Bake at 350° for 1 hour

SUNFLOWER SOUR CREAM

2 cups of water

½ cup sunflower seeds

1 ½ cups hot, cooked millet

2 tsp salt

1/3 cup lemon juice

1. Blend first four ingredients until very very very smooth.

2. Then continue to blend on high as you add lemon juice.